# Using Mi␣

## on the Internet

# BOOKS AVAILABLE

# Using Microsoft Explorer 4 on the Internet

by

**P.R.M. Oliver**
**and**
**N. Kantaris**

BERNARD BABANI (publishing) LTD
THE GRAMPIANS
SHEPHERDS BUSH ROAD
LONDON W6 7NF
ENGLAND

# PLEASE NOTE

Although every care has been taken with the production of this book to ensure that any projects, designs, modifications and/or programs, etc., contained herewith, operate in a correct and safe manner and also that any components specified are normally available in Great Britain, the Publishers and Author(s) do not accept responsibility in any way for the failure (including fault in design) of any project, design, modification or program to work correctly or to cause damage to any equipment that it may be connected to or used in conjunction with, or in respect of any other damage or injury that may be so caused, nor do the Publishers accept responsibility in any way for the failure to obtain specified components.

Notice is also given that if equipment that is still under warranty is modified in any way or used or connected with home-built equipment then that warranty may be void.

© 1999 BERNARD BABANI (publishing) LTD

First Published - January 1999


British Library Cataloguing in Publication Data:

A catalogue record for this book is available from the British Library

ISBN 0 85934 460 6


Cover Design by Gregor Arthur
Cover illustration by Adam Willis
Printed and Bound in Great Britain by The Bath Press, Bath

# ABOUT THIS BOOK

*Using Microsoft Explorer 4 on the Internet* has been written to help you get to grips with the Internet and e-mail in general and with browsing, or surfing, the Web with Microsoft's Internet Explorer in particular.

These days you can't read a paper, listen to the radio, or watch television very long before you hear or see mention of the Internet. It has become an integral part of our lives over the last few years. What importance will it have after the next few years? If it follows the current trend and carries on growing exponentially, it could well become the most important technical development in the history of mankind. So as not to get completely left behind we feel that everyone should test the water, but beware, the Web can be very habit forming.

An attempt has been made not to use too much 'jargon', but with this subject, some is inevitable, so a fairly detailed glossary of terms is included, which should be used with the text where necessary.

The book starts by overviewing the short history of the Internet (from the US military to rampant commercialism) and describes how the Web fits into the general scene.

A chapter follows explaining how you can obtain and install Explorer 4 on your PC, if you do not have Windows 98. How to go about connecting to the Internet and obtaining the technical help that may be needed is also very briefly covered. The book was written using version 4.01 (with Service Pack 1) of the Internet Explorer, working on two PCs under both Windows 95 and Windows 98.

The following chapters describe the current version 4 of Internet Explorer and how best to use it for surfing the Web, including subscriptions, channels and the Active Desktop. Using Outlook Express for handling your e-mail and your Newsgroup activities then follows.

Chapters are included on how to find your way around the Web using some of the many search 'engines' that are available, and how to recognise and guard against some of the unfortunate behaviour traits that have developed with the Internet.

One thing to remember when reading the book is that the whole Internet scenario is changing every day, especially the World Wide Web. What is there to look at today, may have gone, or changed shape, by tomorrow.

The book does not describe how to set up your PC, or how to use Windows. If you need to know more about the Windows environment, then we suggest you select an appropriate book from the 'Books Available' list - these are all published by BERNARD BABANI (publishing) Ltd.

Like the rest of our computer series, this book was written with the busy person in mind. It is not necessary to learn all there is to know about a subject, when reading a few selected pages can usually do the same thing quite adequately. With the help of this book, it is hoped that you will be able to come to terms with the Internet, Microsoft Explorer 4, Outlook Express and the Web and get the most out of your computer in terms of efficiency, productivity and enjoyment, and that you will be able to do it in the shortest, most effective and informative way. Good luck.

If you would like to purchase a Companion Disc for any of the listed books by the same author(s), **apart from this book and the ones marked with an asterisk**, containing the file/program listings which appear in them, then fill in the form at the back of the book and send it to Phil Oliver at the address given.

# ABOUT THE AUTHORS

**Phil Oliver** graduated in Mining Engineering at Camborne School of Mines in 1967 and since then has specialised in most aspects of surface mining technology, with a particular emphasis on computer related techniques. He has worked in Guyana, Canada, several Middle Eastern countries, South Africa and the United Kingdom, on such diverse projects as: the planning and management of bauxite, iron, gold and coal mines; rock excavation contracting in the UK; international mining equipment sales and international mine consulting for a major mining house in South Africa. In 1988 he took up a lecturing position at Camborne School of Mines (part of Exeter University) in Surface Mining and Management. He retired from full-time lecturing in 1998, to spend more time writing, consulting and developing Web sites for clients.

**Noel Kantaris** graduated in Electrical Engineering at Bristol University and after spending three years in the Electronics Industry in London, took up a Tutorship in Physics at the University of Queensland. Research interests in Ionospheric Physics, led to the degrees of M.E. in Electronics and Ph.D. in Physics. On return to the UK, he took up a Post-Doctoral Research Fellowship in Radio Physics at the University of Leicester, and then in 1973 a lecturing position in Engineering at the Camborne School of Mines, Cornwall, (part of Exeter University), where until he retired in 1997 he also assumed the responsibility for the Computing Department.

# ACKNOWLEDGEMENTS

We would like to thank colleagues for the helpful tips and suggestions which assisted us in the writing of this book.

We would also like to thank both Microsoft for making this excellent software available free of charge, or commitment, on the Internet; and PC Plus for supplying it on the CD ROMs that appear with their magazine every month.

# TRADEMARKS

**Arial** and **Times New Roman** are registered trademarks of The Monotype Corporation plc.

**HP and LaserJet** are registered trademarks of Hewlett Packard Corporation.

**IBM** is a registered trademark of International Business Machines, Inc.

**Intel** is a registered trademark of Intel Corporation.

**Microsoft**, **MS-DOS**, **Windows**, **Windows NT**, and **Visual Basic**, are either registered trademarks or trademarks of Microsoft Corporation.

**Netscape Navigator** is a registered trademark of Netscape Communications Corporation.

**PostScript** is a registered trademark of Adobe Systems Incorporated.

**Macintosh, QuickTime** and **TrueType** are registered trademarks of Apple Computer, Inc.

All other brand and product names used in the book are recognised as trademarks, or registered trademarks, of their respective companies.

# CONTENTS

# 1. THE INTERNET

## What is the Internet? - A Brief History

In the mid 1960s with the cold war very prominent in the Northern Hemisphere, the US military faced a strange strategic problem. How could the country successfully communicate after a possible nuclear war? They would need a command and control communication network linking the cities, states and military bases, etc. But, no matter how the network was protected it would always be vulnerable to the impact of a nuclear attack and if the network had a control centre it would be the first to go.

As a solution, the concept was developed that the network itself should be assumed to be unreliable at all times and should be designed to overcome this unreliability. To achieve this, all the nodes of the network would be equal in status, each with its own authority to originate, pass, and receive messages. The messages themselves would be divided into small parts, or packets, with each being separately addressed. The transmission of each packet of data would begin at a specified source node, and end at another specified destination node, but would find its own way through the network, with the route taken being unimportant. With this concept, if sections of the network were destroyed, that wouldn't matter as the packets would use the surviving nodes.

The National Physical Laboratory, here in the UK, set up the first test network on these principles in 1968. Shortly afterwards, the Pentagon's Advanced Research Projects Agency (ARPA) funded a larger, more ambitious project in the USA, with the high-speed 'supercomputers' of the day as the network nodes.

In 1969, the first such node was installed in UCLA. By December of that year, there were four nodes on the infant network, which was named ARPANET, after its sponsor. The four computers could transfer data on dedicated high-speed transmission lines, and could be programmed remotely from the other nodes. For the first time, scientists and researchers could share one another's computer facilities from a long distance. By 1972 there were thirty-seven nodes in ARPANET.

It soon became apparent, however, that much of the traffic on ARPANET was not long-distance computing, but consisted of news and personal messages. Researchers were using ARPANET not only to collaborate on projects and trade ideas on work, but to socialise. They had their own personal accounts on the ARPANET computers, and their own personal addresses for electronic mail and they were very enthusiastic about this particular new service, which we shall hear much more of in later sections.

Throughout the '70s, the ARPA network grew. Its decentralised structure made expansion easy as it could accommodate different types of computers, as long as they could speak the standard packet-switching language. ARPA's original standard for communication was known as NCP short for 'Network Control Protocol', but this was soon superseded by the higher-level standard known as TCP/IP, which has survived until today.

TCP, or 'Transmission Control Protocol', converts messages into streams of packets at the source, then reassembles them back into messages at the destination. IP, or 'Internet Protocol', handles the addressing.

Over the years, ARPANET itself became a smaller and smaller part of the growing proliferation of other networked machines, but TCP/IP linked them all. As the '70s and '80s advanced, many different groups found themselves in possession of powerful computers. It was fairly easy to link these computers to the growing global network. As the use of TCP/IP, which was in the public-domain by that time, became more common, entire other networks were incorporated into the **Internet**.

In 1984 the National Science Foundation became involved and created the new NSFNET linking newer and faster supercomputers with bigger and faster links. Other US government agencies joined the bandwagon, including NASA, the National Institutes of Health and the Department of Energy.

ARPANET itself formally died in 1989, but its functions not only continued but were steadily improved. In Europe, major international 'backbone' networks started to provide connectivity to many millions of computers on a large number of other networks. Commercial network providers in both the US, Europe and Asia were beginning to offer Internet access and support on a competitive basis to any interested parties.

The extended use of the Internet cost the original founders little or nothing extra, since each new node was independent, and had to handle its own technical requirements and funding.

Today there are hundreds of thousands of nodes in the Internet, scattered throughout the world, with more coming on-line all the time and many millions of people using this often named 'Information Super Highway' every day.

Built to be indestructible and with no centralised control, it's no wonder the word 'anarchic' is often bandied around when the Internet is discussed!

## Why Use the Internet?

Now we know what the Internet is, what can we use it for? Five things, basically spring to mind:

- sending and receiving e-mail messages
- taking part in discussion groups
- accessing data stored on distant computers
- transferring data and program files from and to these distant computers
- browsing Web pages.

## E-mail:

Electronic mail has to be one of the main uses of the Internet. It is usually very much faster that letter mail, which is known as 'snailmail' by regular e-mail users. It consists of electronic text, that is transmitted, sometimes in seconds, to anywhere else in the World that is connected to a main network. E-mail can also be used to send software and other types of files which are 'attached' to your message. As we shall see in a later chapter, Internet Explorer software makes this a very easy process.

## Newsgroups:

Discussion groups, or 'newsgroups', are another feature of the Internet that are easily accessed with a good browser like Explorer 4. On the Internet they are generally known as USENET and consist of over 30,000 separate groups which let you freely participate in discussion on a vast amount of subjects. In fact almost any subject you could think of is covered, and the number of groups is growing larger all the time. Unfortunately in some of the groups many of the users seem to consist of adolescent teenagers with very little in the way of common sense or sophistication. You will see what we mean when you try exploring some of the fringe, or *alt* (for alternate) groups.

4

## Long Distance Computing:

As we saw, this was the original inspiration for ARPANET and for some, is still a very important part of the Internet. Using a program like Telnet you can maintain accounts on distant computers, run programs from them as if they were on your own PC, and generally make use of powerful supercomputers a continent away. Most major libraries now offer electronic card catalogues for free search, and CD-ROM archives of specialist data are increasingly available through this type of service.

Most games software is currently available on CD-ROM discs that you run in your own computer, but it is getting common now for game suppliers to also store information that you can access from the Internet.

## File Transfers:

There is a fantastic amount of free software available over the Internet, as well as a multitude of text and graphic files of almost any subject you care to mention.

File transfers carried out with a protocol known as FTP, allow Internet users to access remote machines and retrieve these for their own use. Many Internet computers allow anyone to access them anonymously, and to simply copy their public files, free of charge. With the right connections, entire books can be transferred in a matter of minutes. With the wrong connections though, the process can take hours!

The Internet is in fact spawning a new form of publishing, in which the reader simply electronically copies the work on demand. Several Internet programs, such as 'Archie', 'Gopher' and 'WAIS, have been developed to explore these enormous archives of material, but using the World Wide Web these all become transparent to the end user.

5

# The World Wide Web

Up until fairly recently all of these activities required very expensive computing facilities and a large measure of computer literacy. Times have changed, however, and it is now possible to fairly easily and cheaply install a modem in your PC, connect to the Internet and with a World Wide Web browser, like Microsoft Explorer 4, carry them out with very little technical knowledge. Hence the reason for this book, to help you on your way.

The World Wide Web, WWW, W3, or Web as we shall call it, was initially developed in Switzerland by CERN (the European Laboratory for Particle Physics), to form a distributed hypermedia system. It now consists of Web client computers (yours and mine) and server computers handling multimedia documents with hypertext links built into them. Client computers use browser software (such as Microsoft Explorer) to view pages of these documents, one at a time. Server computers use Web server software to maintain the documents for us to access.

If you have used the Help pages of Windows you are familiar with a hypertext document. It contains links that you click with the mouse pointer to jump to other information. The advantage of hypertext in a Web document is that if you want more information about a particular subject, you just click on it and another page is opened for you to read or look at. In fact, documents can be linked to other documents (or graphics) by completely different authors and stored in completely different computers; much like footnoting, but you can get the referenced document instantly!

So, to access the Web, you run a browser program, in our case Microsoft Explorer, which reads files and documents, and fetches them from other sources on the Internet into the memory of your PC.

Currently the Web offers the following through a hypertext, and in some cases, hypermedia interface:

- HTML-formatted hypertext and hypermedia documents

- Anything served through Gopher

- Anything served through WAIS (Wide-Area Information Servers)

- Anything served through anonymous FTP sites

- Full Archie services (an FTP search service)

- Full Veronica services (a Gopher search service)

- Anything on Usenet

- Anything accessible through Telnet

- Anything in hytelnet (hypertext Telnet)

- Anything in hyper-g (a networked hypertext system in use throughout Europe)

- Anything in the form of man pages (online documentation, or manual, that commonly comes bundled with computers running the UNIX operating system).

Thus Web browsers, such as Explorer, provide users of computer networks with a consistent means to access a variety of media in a very simplified fashion.

They have changed the way people view and create information, and have formed the first true global hypermedia network. No wonder their use has taken off so dramatically in the last two years.

Hypermedia is a superset of hypertext - it is any medium with pointers to other media. This means that the latest browsers display formatted text, images, play sound clips, or even video type animations. Some of these, however, may require extra hardware, like a sound card, in your computer.

## HTML - The Web Language:

You may never get involved with this, but most Web documents are created by authors using a language called HTML (HyperText Markup Language). This offers short codes, or tags, to designate graphical elements and hypertext links. Clicking a link on a Web page in your browser, brings documents located on a distant server to your screen, irrespective of the server's geographic location. Documents may contain text, images, sounds, movies, or a combination of these, in other words - multimedia.

## How Links are Named:

Every link in a hypertext Web document has to have a unique address and for you to use your browser properly you should understand these addresses, or Uniform Resource Locators, (URLs). It is possible to represent nearly any file or service on the Internet with a URL and several example are given below.

The first part of the URL (before the two slashes) specifies the method of access, as described on the next page. The second is typically the domain name of the computer on which the data, or service, is located. Further parts may specify the names of folders and files, the port to connect to, or the text to search for in a database. A URL is always a single unbroken line with **no spaces**.

Here are some examples of URLs:

**http://www.ex.ac.uk/location/book.html**

This would connect to an HTTP server (in this case a Web server at the University of Exeter) and would retrieve an HTML file (a Web file).

**ftp://www.xerox.com/pub/file.txt**

This would open an FTP connection to www.xerox.com and retrieve a text file.

**gopher://www.hcc.hawaii.edu**

This would connect to the Gopher at the distant www.hcc.hawaii.edu (A university in Hawaii).

**file://www.ex.ac.uk/location/pic.gif**

This would retrieve a picture file and display it.

**file://www.ex.ac.uk/location/**

This would display the directory contents of a distant location.

**news:alt.sex**

This would read the latest Usenet news by connecting to a specified news host and would return the articles in the alt.sex newsgroup in hypermedia format.

The first part of the URL (before the two slashes) gives the method of access at that address:

- **http** - a hypertext document or directory

- **Gopher** - a gopher document or menu

- **ftp** - a file available for downloading or a directory of such files

- **news** - a newsgroup

- **Telnet -** a computer system that you can log into from across the Internet

- **WAIS** - a database or document on a WAIS (**W**ide **A**rea **I**nformation **S**earch) database

- **file** - a file located on a local drive (like your hard drive)

Sites that run World Wide Web servers are typically named with a www. at the beginning of the network address.

As we shall see, Microsoft Explorer allows you to specify a URL and thus connect to that document, or service. When selecting hypertext links in a Web page (an HTML document), you are actually sending a request to open a URL. In this way, hyperlinks can be made not only to other texts and media, but also to other network services. Web browsers are not simply Web clients, but are also full FTP, Gopher, and Telnet clients in their own rights.

All of these features are now easily available over ordinary phone lines, once you get direct Internet access through a local Internet Service Provider (ISP), as explained in the next chapter.

# 2. INTERNET EXPLORING

At the time of writing this book, the Web browser market for Windows PCs had two main players, Netscape and Microsoft. Browsers are now being given away by both of these. Netscape started the trend by posting beta, or test, copies of versions of its Netscape Navigator for free download. Then it effectively made the shipping version of its browsers free downloads as well, by allowing 90 days for evaluation. To get into the market, Microsoft gives away all its browser products, as well as including Explorer 4 as part of the Windows 98 package.

These companies originally rushed to give away very high quality software because they saw a lot of money to be made in the future. By flooding the market with their Navigator software, Netscape were able to float their company on the US stock market in record time and saw its stock price rocket to rather excessive heights. This without making a profit until after it went public and with what looked like a very unimpressive balance sheet. The fact that at the time it was the dominant player in the Internet market was enough for Wall Street. The situation now is somewhat different as Netscape are fighting to survive.

Microsoft have made a habit of dominating their markets. Look at DOS, Windows and then the applications like Excel and Word, etc. The Web browser market is going the same way. At the time of writing about half the people who visit our Web sites now use a version of Explorer, compared to about 25% only a year ago.

We hope there will be enough room for both of these two major players. Having used both of their current browsers, we feel that Microsoft's version 4 is technically ahead. Having said that, there are features in both that we like. As usual, nothing is perfect!

## Microsoft Products

At the time of writing, Microsoft have versions of their Internet Explorer 4 available for use on all the popular computer operating systems. This scenario is changing quickly and a beta version of Explorer 5 is imminent, but our book was written using the current version 4.01 for Windows 95 and Windows 98.

As well as including it with Windows 98, Microsoft offers Internet Explorer 4 for the Windows 3.1, Windows 95, and Windows NT platforms, as well as for Macintosh and Unix.

## Internet Explorer Requirements

The minimum hardware requirements to run Internet Explorer 4 depend on the version of Windows you are using:

### Windows 3.1

A 486, or higher, PC with 12 MB of RAM (but as much as possible is recommended), a VGA Display (SVGA with 256 colours or higher is recommended), and at least 25 MB of hard disc space.

### Windows 95

A 486, or higher, PC with 12 MB of RAM (but as much as possible is recommended), a VGA Display (SVGA with 256 colours or higher is recommended), and at least 50 MB of hard disc space.

### Windows NT

A standard installation with Windows NT4 requires 24 MB of RAM and at least 50 MB of hard disc space.

You also need a connection to the Internet, via a Modem, Ethernet Card, or ISDN direct phone line.

To run Explorer 4 as an on-line browser you must have a direct 32-bit Internet connection. The ability to send and receive e-mail does not necessarily mean you will be able to access the Web. There are three requirements for this:

1   A direct Ethernet connection to the net, or a dialup SLIP or PPP account from an Internet service provider.

2   A 32-bit TCP/IP stack.

3   The Microsoft Explorer software.

## Getting On Line

Unless you are lucky enough to have a PC which is connected to a Local Area Network (LAN) which has Internet access, you will need a modem to be able to communicate with the rest of the world. This is a device that converts data so that it can be transmitted over the telephone system.

You will also need to find, and subscribe to, a suitable Internet provider. There are many such providers in the UK. Most can be listed on the Web by accessing the following address:

**http://thelist.internet.com/**

and looking under the UK, or wherever else you are based. Another way would be to buy an Internet based PC magazine from your local newsagent and look at the reviews and adverts. Also you could try your telephone directory, or possibly adverts in the computer section of your local paper. Be careful though before committing yourself to one provider as the quality of service and costs can vary considerably.

One thing we can't do here is make specific recommendations, but try and find someone who uses the company you decide on, or have a trial period with them.

What you are ideally looking for is **full dial-up SLIP or PPP connection with unlimited WWW access to the Internet**, and this should be possible by dialling a local number to your provider's access point. (SLIP and PPP are only two communication standards that you need to have, but do not need to understand).

The local call access will mean your phone bills should not be excessive, especially if you do your Web accessing in off-peak times. The unlimited access means you will not pay any extra to your Internet Provider no matter how many hours you spend on line, just your monthly fee.

A service, like that described above, will probably cost in the region of £10 per month, and there may well be a setting up charge as well. You may be lucky and get it even cheaper, there is a lot of competition.

**From now on in this book, we assume that you have an active connection to the Internet. Trouble shooting this is not within our remit!**

## Getting Your Browser

If you already have your version of Explorer 4 up and running on your computer you can skip the rest of this section. If not, you will need to obtain the software. When you are actually connected to the Internet you can download  Microsoft's Internet Explorer software absolutely free from their Web site at:

**http://www.microsoft.com**

If you are not yet connected, you obviously can't do this, but there is a better way now anyway. Some computer magazines that come with CD-ROMs carry

Web browsers on them. Our favourite is PC Plus, which includes, every month, the latest browsers from both Netscape and Microsoft. With the size of these browsers this can save many hours of valuable time downloading. The saving in your phone bill may well pay for the magazine as well. One thing to remember though with both sources is to select the version of Explorer designed for your operating system.

## Installing Internet Explorer:

If you have downloaded the program, simply double-clicking the downloaded .EXE program file from a Windows 95 'My Computer' window, or the Program Manager of Windows 3.1, will start the installation procedure. From the CD-ROM just follow the instructions and click **Next** to continue.

We were first confronted with the above welcome message, followed by the licence agreement. As long as you are happy with this, accepting it starts the procedure.

In the next window you select the type of installation. We chose a Standard one as shown here.

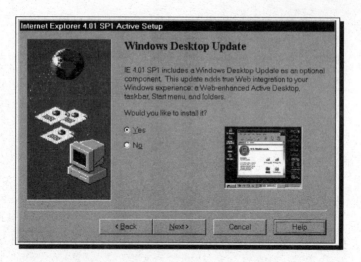

If you are using Windows 95, the main choice to make is whether to 'go the whole hog' and install the Windows Desktop Update. This modifies most of the Windows visual features and makes Windows 95 almost the same as Windows 98 to use. If you have plenty of memory, and you like making changes, this will be for you. If you don't like the resulting interface, you can always remove it in the **Add/Remove Programs** window opened with the **Start**, **Settings**, **Control Panel** commands.

When you have chosen a location for the program on your PC, the file copy process is started which proceeds for several minutes while the program is installed and your system is reconfigured. When this procedure is finished you will be asked to restart your computer by clicking the **OK** button. Another long wait follows so you need to be patient with this installation. If you did not have enough space on your hard disc, you will be told to free up more room and try again. Good luck.

When you regain control you will find your desktop has changed somewhat. If you have any shortcut icons they will probably have been completely re-arranged, at least two new icons and a Channel Guide will have

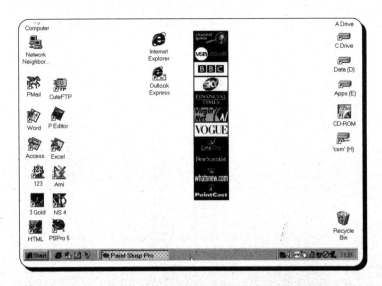

been added, and the Taskbar will have a Quick Launch bar the same as that with Windows 98. All of these are shown above, after we had sorted out the shortcuts a little.

## The Channel Bar:

With Explorer 4 a channel is a special type of Web site which delivers its content 'automatically' from the Internet to your computer. These are set up mostly by large organisations and with them you don't see just a Web page, you also get a rich map of the Web site, which enables you to quickly select and view the content you want.

We will spend more time on channels in Chapter 6, but if you want to experiment with the new Active  Channel bar on your Desktop, go ahead. If not, you can remove it by clicking the X button on the bar which opens at the top when you move the pointer over the bar.

## Starting Internet Explorer

Internet
Explorer

Double-clicking the Internet Explorer icon, shown here, will open the browser. The first time you do this it will probably start the Internet Connection Wizard, which steps you through the process of establishing your link to the Internet.

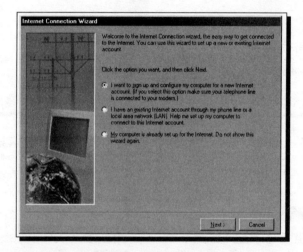

This Wizard can make the process of setting up your connection quite painless. We were very pleased to see that facilities for connecting up via a Local Area Network are now included. Obviously how you complete the options that are offered will depend on your particular system and circumstances. Before starting this operation be sure to find out from your system administrator or your Internet Service Provider exactly what settings you will need to enter.

When the Wizard has finished its work you will be asked if you want to make this your default, or main, browser. Clicking **Yes** will set the file association of Web page files so that they will always open into this particular browser.

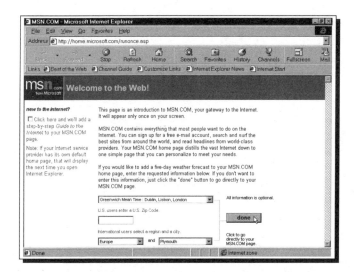

After all this procedure you then get your first look at the new browser. If all is well, you should get an opening screen which may look something like that shown above. What appears will depend on Microsoft and will probably change fairly often.

Note that when the Explorer is actually downloading data from the network, the Status Indicator to the right of the menu bar shows with an active display, and the status bar gives an indication of what is actually happening.

The opening screen shown here is really an advert for MSN, a service provided by Microsoft. They would rather you spent all your time working in their territory!

## Your PC Settings

Before we go any further, a few words on screen display resolutions may be useful. Your computer may well have started life set to a screen resolution of 640 x 480 pixels. It then displays a screen of 640 pixels wide and 480 pixels high on the monitor. The bigger the

19

monitor you have, the bigger the screen resolution you can use, as everything gets smaller as the resolution goes up.

For Web browsing you want as large a resolution as you can get so that you can fit more on the screen. Web pages are almost always too large to fit on one screen. We recommend using a resolution of 800 x 600 if you have a 14" or 15" monitor, and a resolution of 1024 x 768 for 17" and larger monitors.

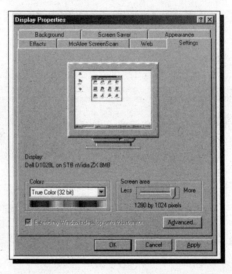

It is easy to change the screen settings, but Windows may have to be re-started for them to take effect. Click the **Start**, button, and then **Settings**, **Control Panel,** double-click on the **Display** icon, and then click the Settings tab to open the window shown here. Another way to open this box is to right-click on the Desktop and select **Properties** from the opened menu. The details above were for one of our PCs, yours may well be different. Both the **Colors** and the **Screen area** slider settings are interlinked. The higher the colour setting the lower will be the maximum Desktop area, or resolution. In our case above with a True Colour (32 bit) setting our maximum resolution is 1280 by 1024.

With this colour setting, you get near photographic image quality, and many graphics, or pictures, look much better than with only a 256 colour setting. You will find the Web much more entertaining if you surf with thousand, or millions, of colours, instead of 256.

## A Trial Run

You should now be up and running with the Internet Explorer 4, so let's do something. There are many millions of Web pages to look at, so where do we start? You may have started already from the last MSN page, but there is one UK institution that we all know and love, the Government! They have spent time and money on their Web presentations, so we will take a quick look.

Start Explorer, if it is not already going, and click the Search button shown here (on the button bar known as the Toolbar). This opens the Search panel on the left of the Explorer window, which should be similar to that shown on the right.

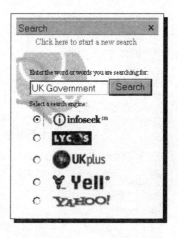

We will discuss Web searches again in a later chapter, so for now type 'UK Government' in the text box, and select **infoseek**, as we did here.

Clicking the **Search** button opens an InfoSeek search page in the panel, and searches for references to the 'UK Government', the first entry of which is shown on the next page. InfoSeek is just one of the many search utilities available for finding your way round the Web.

InfoSeek was aware of 5,743 relevant Web pages, and brought details of what it considered to be the most relevant ones to the screen. Search tools are very powerful and useful facilities, which we shall discuss more of in a later chapter.

In our case the first entry above will do. Clicking the underlined link <u>CCTA's Government Information Service</u> will open the home page we were looking for, as shown on the right above.

If we had known the URL address (which is also given in the search details) we could have typed it straight into the **Address** bar, as follows:

```
http://www.open.gov.uk/
```

This would also have opened the same Web page when the Enter key on the keyboard was pressed. Quite a colourful display, but where is the menu?

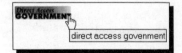

Try moving the mouse pointer around the screen. When it passes over some of the screen items it changes to a hand, as shown in our illustration.

That means each of these graphics is actually a link to another Web page. The status bar, at the bottom of the screen, shows the URL address of the link pointed to. Clicking any of these links on the page will open another page, which may well contain more links.

We will leave it to you to explore this site further. You may find some interesting information, or on the other hand, it may help to send you to sleep.

**NOTE** - If a Web page is taking a long time to load you can open another browser window with the **File**, **New**, **Window** command, or the <Ctrl+N> keystroke shortcut. You can have as many Web pages open at the same time as your computer's memory will hold, all doing different things.

# 3. BASIC PROGRAM FEATURES

## Explorer Screen Layout

The illustration below shows an empty Internet Explorer 4 window with the Toolbars maximised by dragging the bottom borders down as far as they will go.

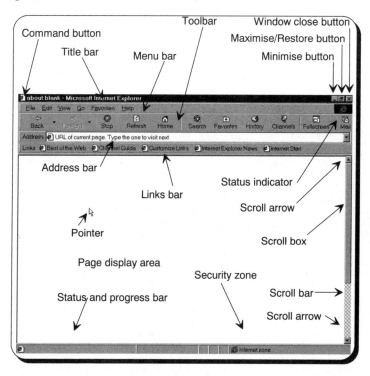

It is perhaps worth spending some time looking at the various parts that make up this window, which is subdivided into several areas with the following functions:

| *Area* | *Function* |
|---|---|
| Command button | Clicking on this program icon button, located in the upper-left corner of each window, displays the pull-down Control menu which can be used to control the window. It includes commands for restoring, maximising, minimising, moving, sizing, and closing the window; and for switching on and off the display of the Tool and Status bars. |
| Title bar | The bar which displays the title of the current Web page. |
| Menu bar | The bar which allows you to choose from several menu options. Clicking on a menu item displays the pull-down menu associated with that item. |
| Minimise button | The button you point to and click to reduce an application to an icon on the Taskbar. |
| Restore button | The button you point to and click to restore the window to its former size. When that happens, the Restore button changes to a Maximise button which is used to fill the screen with the active window. |
| Close button | The X button that you click to close the window. |
| Toolbar | A bar of icons that you click to carry out some of the more common Explorer actions. |
| Address bar | Shows the location of the current page, or the URL of the new page to go to next. |

| | |
|---|---|
| Links bar | These automatically load on-line Web pages and can be set up with your own favourite links. |
| Status indicator | Shows when data transfer is taking place. |
| Page display | The main body of the window that displays Web pages. |
| Explorer bar | A vertical bar in the left side of the browser window that opens when the Search, Favorites, History and Channels Toolbar buttons are actioned. (Not shown on the previous page) |
| Scroll bars | If the contents of a window will not fit in it, scroll bars are added to the right and/or the bottom of the window. |
| Scroll arrows | The arrowheads at each end of a scroll bar which you can click to scroll the screen up and down, or left and right. |
| Scroll box | Dragging this box up or down the scroll bar will rapidly scroll through a Web page. |
| Status bar | The animated bar that shows the progress of a downloading operation and the address of the link or graphic, pointed to by the mouse. |
| Security zone | Shows the security settings for the Web site being accessed. |

As is now becoming a standard feature with Microsoft programs, at first glance an empty Explorer window can look a little grey and lifeless, but when you move the mouse pointer over the toolbar its buttons 'light up' when they are active. This is a very pleasing feature, the window being designed not to detract from the Web pages being viewed in it.

## Menu Bar Options

Each option on the menu bar has associated with it a pull-down sub-menu. This follows the normal Windows convention, so to access the menu, either click the mouse on an option, or press the <Alt> key, which causes the first option of the menu (in this case **File**) to be highlighted, then use the arrow keys to highlight any of the options in the menu. Pressing either the <Enter> key, or the left mouse button, reveals the pull-down sub-menu of the highlighted menu option. The sub-menu of the **File** option is shown here.

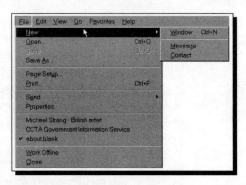

Menu options can also be activated directly by pressing the <Alt> key followed by the underlined letter of the required option. Thus pressing <Alt+F>, also opens the sub-menu of **File**.

You can use the up and down arrow keys to move the highlighted bar up and down a sub-menu, or the right and left arrow keys to move along the options in the Menu bar. Pressing the <Enter> key selects the highlighted option or executes the highlighted command. Pressing the <Esc> key once, closes the pull-down sub-menu, while pressing the <Esc> key for a second time, closes the Menu system.

Note that those commands which are not available at any specific time will be inactive and appear on the menu in a lighter colour. In our example on the facing page the option **Save** is not available.

## Keyboard Shortcuts:

Some of the menu options have keyboard shortcuts attached to them. These are very useful to people who are more used to the keyboard than the mouse. In the **File** sub-menu there are several. For example, pressing <Ctrl+N>, the 'N' key with the 'Ctrl' key also depressed, will open a new browser window.

We have listed the available shortcuts in Appendix A.

## Mouse Right-Click Menu

You can use your right mouse button to click objects on a page and see a drop-down shortcut, or context, menu, with contents that depend on what you click:

| | |
|---|---|
| On a link | The menu items refer to the page specified by the link. |
| On an image | They refer to the image file specified by the image. |
| On background | They apply to the current page, its text, or its background image. |
| On the Title bar | They allow you to control the current window. |
| On the Toolbar | The menu items help you customise the Toolbar area. |

This example shows the options that were available when the mouse was right-clicked on the photograph.

The actions available were; opening the page linked to the image in the current window, or in a new one, saving the linked page to a file on disc, or sending it to the printer; saving the picture to a file on disc, or setting it as the Windows wallpaper; copying the image or its URL to the clipboard; and adding the linked file to the Favourites list. Clicking on **Properties** would show details of the image file.

As usual, unavailable options are shown in grey.

## The Toolbar

Most Windows applications are now fully equipped with a Toolbar option, and Internet Explorer is no exception. It contains a series of buttons that you can click with your mouse pointer to quickly carry out a program function.

The button functions are pretty self-explanatory and are as follows:

| Button | Function |
|---|---|
| **Back** | Displays the previous page viewed, or selects from the drop-down history list. |
| **Forward** | Displays the next page viewed, or selects from the drop-down history list. |
| **Stop** | Halts any on-line transfer of page data. |
| **Refresh** | Brings a fresh copy of the current Web page to the viewer. |
| **Home** | Displays your specified home page, with a Microsoft page as the default. |
| **Search** | Opens the Explorer bar with access to Microsoft selected search facilities. |
| **Favorites** | Opens the Explorer bar with access to your saved favourite sites, or bookmarks. |
| **History** | Opens the Explorer bar and displays a hierarchical list of the Web pages you have previously viewed. |
| **Channels** | Opens the Explorer bar to display a list of available channels. |
| **Fullscreen** | Sets the browser to display a full screen view but leaving a customisable Toolbar for viewing control. A new and superb feature. |
| **Mail** | Gives quick access to your e-mail and Newsgroup facilities. |
| **Font** | Gives a choice of 5 font sizes and of foreign fonts for the browser to use. An optional button. |
| **Print** | Prints the open Web page, or frame, using the current print settings. |
| **Edit** | Opens the current Web page in the default HTML editor, or Microsoft Word. |

If the Toolbar is not showing when a window is opened, you simply open the **View** menu, select the **Toolbars** option and choose what features you want to show. This places a tick '√' character on the selected options. Selecting them again in the future, will toggle the option off. You might want to remove parts of the Toolbar to get more viewing area, or because you do not intend to use them.

## Layout of the Control Area:

If, like us, you find the Toolbar buttons a little on the large side you can change the way they appear on your screen. Right-clicking an empty section of the Toolbar and de-selecting the **Text Labels** option will remove the text and bring the icons closer together. We go one step further by selecting **Small icons** in the Advanced settings sheet opened with the **View**, **Internet Options** command, as shown below.

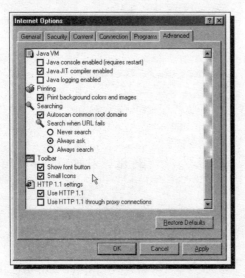

This is also where you switch on the Font button. It is worthwhile experimenting with the settings here to find out which way you prefer your browser to operate.

Our example here shows the difference in the size of icons after these operations have been carried out. The 'before' and 'after' sections of the Toolbar are both displayed at the same scale.

With Explorer 4, you can also alter the layout of the Control bars by dragging the bars up or down with the mouse pointer, as shown in the sequence below. The control area shrinks as you drag the frame up and expands again when it is dragged down.

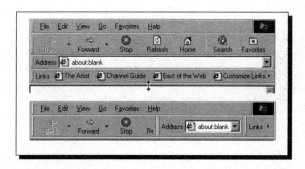

You can also try different combinations of controls in the same bars by dragging the vertical embossed lines between them. We show below our favourite arrangement, which includes all the important features, but takes up the minimum of screen space.

This is really a very clever feature, which lets you arrange the control area to suit the way you work. It will take a few minutes of experimenting though.

## The Address Bar

The address field shows you the location (or URL address) of the current page being viewed. If you know the URL of the next page you want to look at, you can type it into this field. Simply pressing the <Enter> key will load the page.

A pull-down menu, opened by clicking the down-arrow at the right of the field, lets you choose from the most recent locations you have entered, which can save some typing!

## The Links Bar

Under the Address bar there is a set of Links buttons which, by default, open various on-line pages prepared for you by Microsoft and kept at their site. These links are well worth exploring and may give you some ideas about where to go on the Web, and indeed, what can be usefully achieved instead of just surfing aimlessly from one link to another.

As an example, we show on the next page what was in the 'Best of the Web' page the last time we visited Microsoft's site. This will almost certainly have changed by the time this gets to you!

The Links buttons do not have to stay pointing to Microsoft's pages. You can easily set them to hold your own most used sites, as is described in the next chapter.

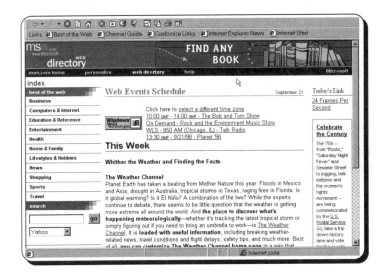

Each entry in the Index list above is in fact a link to another Microsoft Web page. These give you lots of links to explore (by clicking them with the mouse), and each one almost certainly has many more links built into it.

There is always something new, just over the horizon, on the Web.

## Fullscreen View

A new and very welcome feature to Explorer 4 is the option to browse using a full screen view. We often  view the Web with several windows open at the same time, and so that we can see them all they obviously have to be reduced in size. When you want to look at one page in more detail, clicking the Fullscreen icon on the Toolbar shows it using the whole screen, except for a thin Toolbar along the top edge, and reduced scroll bars if necessary. Even the Toolbar can be customised by right-clicking it. With the screen resolution we use, we can get the Toolbar icons, the Menu bar and the Address bar onto the Fullscreen Toolbar. We usually have **Auto Hide** selected as well, so that the Toolbar itself only displays when you move the pointer over it. The rest of the time the Web page is displayed with no Windows 'clutter' at all, as in our example below.

This option really makes viewing Web pages a pleasure. For this alone, it would be worth converting to Explorer 4! Clicking the Fullscreen icon again returns you to the window layout you had before.

## General Option Settings

Like most Windows programs, you control the other ways Internet Explorer operates for you, by changing settings in a series of tabbed sheets accessed with the **View**, **Internet Options** menu command, as we saw earlier. Perhaps we should now look at some of the options available here.

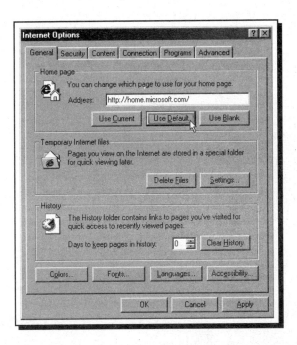

In the **General** tab sheet, shown open above, you can control which page is loaded when you start Explorer, or click the Home icon. We are sure you will not want the Microsoft default option, so we suggest you load the page you do want before you open this dialogue box and then select the **Use Current** option.

The **Temporary Internet files** options let you control the hard disc cache where the program stores all the files it downloads. The **History** section gives you some control over the details of the pages you have recently visited which are displayed when you click the History Toolbar icon. If you ever run short of hard disc space, clearing these two options will release that space being used for temporary file storage.

The **Fonts** and **Languages** buttons let you set the default fonts and language used by your browser, and the **Accessibility** button lets you override any font size, colour or type settings made in a Web page. This is not usually a good thing to do, unless you have very strong preferences, as Web page authors usually spend a lot of time specifying their page settings to get the visual effects they want.

The **Colors** button gives you control of the colours in a Web page. We suggest you leave the **Use Windows colors** option selected here, but select **Use hover color** as shown below.

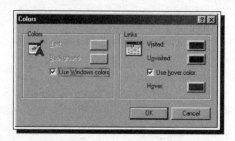

With 'hover' colour set, as shown, the links on a Web page change colour to a bright red whenever you pass the pointer over them.

While you are at it, take a good look around the other options on the other tabbed sheets. If an option is not self explanatory, you can click the help button shown here ![?] (which is located in the top right of the window), then click the 'What's this' pointer on the offending item to get more details of its function, as shown here on the right.

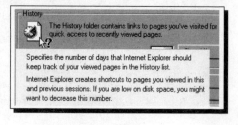

## Saving Pictures

For many people, one of the big attractions of the Internet is the enormous collection of photographs and other graphical data that is freely available. Whatever your preferences, all you have to do is search until you find what you are looking for.

But how can I download a picture onto my PC and have it to look at, whenever I want? I hear you asking.

If you have followed this chapter up to this point you will not need to ask, you will probably be doing it already. If not, the procedure is very easy. Once you have found the picture you want on a Web page, simply right-click your mouse on it and select from the object menu that opens.

Our example here, shows a photograph of one of our consultants surveying, with the right-click menu options that are available. Clicking on **Save Picture As...** will open the Save As dialogue box for you to enter the **File name** and folder to **Save in** details. When you have done this, simply click the **Save** button to capture your picture. Don't fill up your hard disc though!

## Explorer Help

The trend these days is for programs to be shipped with very little in the way of a manual and a much less detailed built-in Help system than was the norm a few years ago. We shouldn't really complain about this as maybe that is why you are reading this book!

Internet Explorer has a built-in Help system, which is accessed with the **Help**, **Contents and Index** menu command. This opens a Windows 98 type Help window, as shown below.

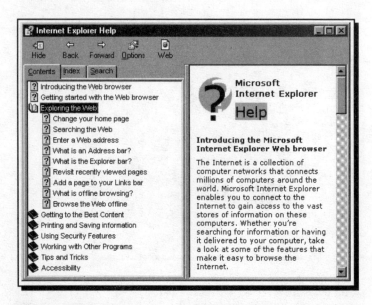

We strongly recommend that you work your way through all the listed items. Clicking on a closed book icon will open it and display a listing of its contents. Double-clicking on a list item will open a window with a few lines of Help information.

Another way of browsing the Help system is to click the **Index** tab and work your way through the alphabetic listing. The **Search** tab opens a search

40

facility you can use, as shown below. In this example we typed 'saving pictures' in the **Type in the keyword to find** text field and clicked the **List Topics** button. Then, selecting one of the **Topic**s found and clicking **Display**, opened Help information on it.

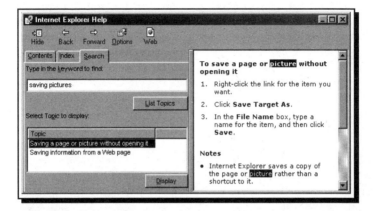

The Help provided by Microsoft with version 4 of the browser is a big improvement over the previous version.

Help and other facilities are also available that can be downloaded from the menu options shown below. These, of course, expect you to have your Internet connection open.

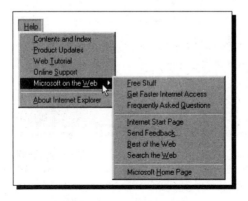

## Updating your Browser:

The **Help**, **Product Updates** command opens the Microsoft Windows Update page, which if you let it, will check out your system and suggest what upgrades are available for downloading. These will be automatically installed for you. Nice and easy at the time, but with no back-up files you may have problems if you ever have to re-install your software.

## An On-line Tutorial:

The basic on-line Web tutorial, shown below, can be accessed from the **Help** menu, with the **Web Tutorial** command. If you are new to it, this may well be a good place to start your Web browsing, but it can be a little slow at times, depending on the amount of traffic crossing the Atlantic.

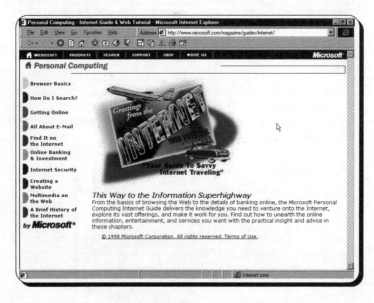

# 4. MORE SKILLS AND FEATURES

## Some Starting Sites

As we saw in the last chapter, Microsoft have provided a starting page for your Web browsing. This is, as you would expect, a really professional page with point and click links to other pages of interest. You can even customise to show the type of information you are interested in, and then make it your home page.

You can also see in our screen dump above, an example of the advertising that is becoming more of a feature on many Web pages. The search engine pages also seem to be getting weighed down with it. Generating advertising revenue almost certainly helps to pay for some of our 'free' Web facilities, but at the expense of speed. Every graphic has to be downloaded and takes valuable time.

## A Useful Site:

When you get fed up with surfing between sites which offer all manner of visual and audio entertainment, you might like to visit one useful page we recently found. Try entering the following address, which points to an American University site, so hopefully it will stay active. But don't forget things can change overnight on the Web.

**http://www.ithaca.edu/Library/Training/useful.html**

The header of this page is shown below. It is maintained by a librarian and points to an interesting array of reference and other kinds of library oriented sites.

---

### ICYouSee:

### What Can You Do On the WORLD WIDE WEB That Is Actually Useful?

Back to the ICYouSee Index?

One criticism of the Web is that it is just a big toy that is mostly good for wasting time. But mixed in with the strange and weird are some **useful** resources. Useful, I realize, can mean many things. For the purpose of this page, I'm limiting the definition of "useful" to **"designed to promote research or support an academic curriculum."** On this page I have tried to put together representative samples of some resources. The purpose is to be selective and illustrative, rather than exhaustive.

---

## Using Web Information

Once you have found what you were looking for on the Web you can, with very little in the way of basic skills, save it to your own PC and use it for your own purposes. Every Web page consists of HTML code, text, graphic or video images, sound files, or links to files of some sort that have been used in the page construction. All of these can be saved for your own use, as we shall see.

## The Mouse Pointer:

You have almost certainly noticed by now that the mouse pointer changes shape depending on what part of a page it is pointing to. There are three main shapes:

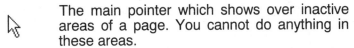

The main pointer which shows over inactive areas of a page. You cannot do anything in these areas.

The hand pointer that appears when you move over a link. Clicking the right mouse button opens a menu of actions you can carry out with that link, or its file.

The I beam pointer that means you can select the text beneath it.

## Copying Text:

You can copy selected, or highlighted, text from an Explorer page to the Windows clipboard with the **Edit**, **Copy** menu command, or the <Ctrl+C> shortcut. If you want to copy all the text on a page, it is quicker to select it with the <Ctrl+A> keyboard shortcut, or the **Edit**, **Select All** command. The copied text will have all of the HTML tags stripped out.

Once the text you want is on the clipboard, you can **Paste** it, <Ctrl+V>, into whatever open Windows application program you want, and then save it. Notepad is useful for this, or WordPad for a lot of text. But remember, the text might look formatted in WordPad, but this is only done with imported space characters. In either case, you will almost certainly have to do some editing to remove lots of unwanted empty spaces.

## Viewing Source Code:

If you want to see what the code for any page actually looks like, you can use the **View**, **Source** command. This opens the file in Notepad, so you can edit it as well and save it wherever you want, except back to its Web site, of course. Our example below shows some of the actual HTML source code for the Web page displayed in the illustration on page 36.

```
   <TITLE>Michael Strang - British artist - landscapes, seascapes,
portraits and flowers</TITLE>
   <META NAME="GENERATOR" CONTENT="">
   <META NAME="Author" CONTENT="Phil Oliver">
   <META NAME="Description" CONTENT="Site of Michael Strang, the
contemporary British artist and oil painter of seascapes, landscapes,
portraits and flowers. An exhibition of over 80 drawings and paintings,
with some art for sale and a limited edition print issue.">
   <META NAME="KeyWords" CONTENT="artist, landscape, dandelions, seascape,
Michael Strang, picture, oil  painting, prints for sale, Michael Strang,
Cornwall, Cornish art, painter, English, British, limited edition print,
portrait, poppy, poppies, Penzance, Gulval, contemporary art, exhibition,
gallery, galleries, flowers, sunflowers, cornfield, Royal Academy, Tate,
still life, commissions, St Ives, Porthmeor beach, canvas, museum,
contemporary, still life">

<script language="javascript">
function GotoURL(f) {
        top.location.href = f.picker.options[f.picker.selectedIndex].value;
        }
</script>
```

## Saving a Whole Page:

The **File**, **Save As** menu command lets you save the current Explorer page with all the HTML codes still in place. A page saved in this way does not retain its graphics, only the text and codes. Make sure, if you want to use the page again with your browser, that you save it with the default .htm extension.

There are several reasons for wanting to save a whole Web page to disc:

- So that you can edit the source code to form the basis of a page of your own.

46

- To create a hypertext 'reference book' of pages you have down-loaded. This would work on any PC that had the files on it.

- To use embedded links in a file as instant Bookmarks.

## Saving a Target Link:

Explorer has another way of saving a Web file without you even having to open it. If you right-click your mouse pointer on a link in an open page, an object menu is opened, as we have seen before.

Selecting the **Save Target As** option from this menu, and completing the details of file name and destination folder in the **Save As** box, will start the download process. While the actual download is taking place a window like this is opened. This usually has a progress bar that indicates how the process is proceeding, and shows an estimate of the remaining time that will be taken.

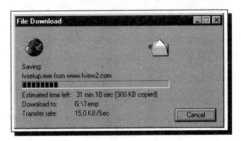

## Downloading a Program File

If you capture many graphics you may well need a program to quickly view and manipulate them. One of the best shareware programs we have come across to do this is LView Pro, and as an example we will step you through the process of downloading this from the Internet.

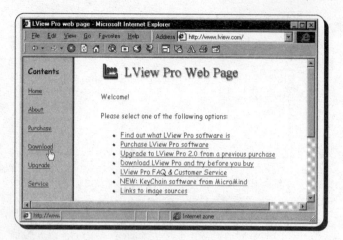

To open the home page, shown above, type the following URL in the Address field and press <Enter>:

**http://www.lview.com/**

Clicking the <u>Download</u> link opens a page with some details of how to download the program.

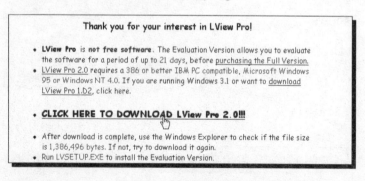

If you want, you can action the **Click here to DOWNLOAD...** link to start the process, which is in fact an FTP operation.

The warning box shown next is opened to make you aware that there is a danger of importing viruses if you download program files from an unknown source. The provider of this program should be a safe source, so

make
the **Save this
program to
disk** option is
selected and
click the **OK**
button.

Complete
the details in
the **Save As**
dialogue box,
(we suggest
you save it to
a temporary folder called **Temp**), and click **Save** to
start downloading. The File Download box is opened,
as shown on page 47, and as long as this box is open the downloading is still taking place. A flurry of disc activity and the display of this message indicates the completion of the operation.

To check that the file has been received on your

system, open the **Temp** folder in a 'My Computer' window, and you should see it there as shown in our example on the left.

If you want to find out more about the file you could right-click the mouse pointer on its icon and select the **Properties** option from the opened menu. This opens the tabbed shown below, which gives two pages of the file.

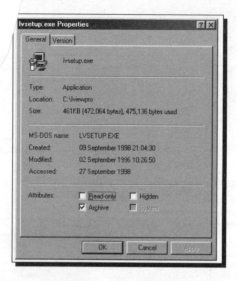

As you may well know, most objects in Windows 95 and 98 have properties, which you can examine and sometimes change in dialogue box panes like this.

Once you have followed the on-line instructions and installed LView Pro you will have a very useful graphic utility program to evaluate. Of course, as it is shareware, if you carry on using it you should be prepared to pay the $30 registration fee.

## Saving with Graphics

Although all the graphics and text code for a down-loaded Web page are actually saved in a cache on your hard disc you cannot simply copy these to another PC and view complete Web pages there. The link codings on the HTML page will not be correct. To save Explorer pages with their graphics embedded you need extra software to sort out this problem.

A favourite site of ours for finding extra Internet software is run by TUCOWS Interactive Limited, and it is well worth taking a look at one of their sites. If you are thinking of downloading anything from the Internet you should try and find the nearest site to you that you can so as to save on downloading time. Tucows (sorry about the name) have a mirror site at Lancaster University at the following address:

**http://micros.hensa.ac.uk/tucows/**

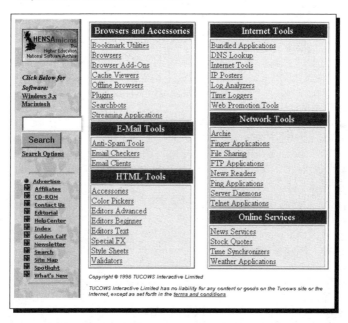

Copyright © 1998 TUCOWS Interactive Limited

TUCOWS Interactive Limited has no liability for any content or goods on the Tucows site or the Internet, except as set forth in the terms and conditions

Our screen dump above shows an edited version of some of the software types available when we selected the 'Win 95/98' option from the opening Tucows screen.

A few minutes looking around this site is well worth anybody's time. You can find some very powerful and free programs to download and try out.

## Printing Web Pages

It was originally thought by some, that computers would lead to the paperless office. That has certainly not proved to be correct. It seems that however good our electronic communication media becomes most people want to see the results printed on paper. As far as books are concerned, long may that last!

Microsoft have built into Explorer 4 the ability to produce the best printed output of Web pages we have so far seen. Pages with frames are handled and you can also control the headers and footers that are printed. The screen layout of most Web pages depends on the size of the window you have open and the font size you are using. Try this out by viewing a text-based page full screen and then reducing it to a smaller window. The page will be reformatted around any embedded graphics. The same thing happens when you print, except that the paper size, not the window, determines the eventual layout.

Before you print, you should check the page settings with the **File**, **Page Setup** command, which opens the dialogue box shown here. The usual options of page **Size** and **Source**, **Margins** and **Orientation** are controlled here, as well as the new ones, **Header** and **Footer**. The Help

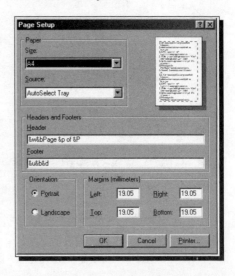

section, shown on the next page is perhaps the easiest way to come to terms with how to use these.

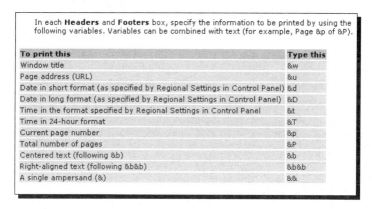

In each **Headers** and **Footers** box, specify the information to be printed by using the following variables. Variables can be combined with text (for example, Page &p of &P).

| To print this | Type this |
|---|---|
| Window title | &w |
| Page address (URL) | &u |
| Date in short format (as specified by Regional Settings in Control Panel) | &d |
| Date in long format (as specified by Regional Settings in Control Panel) | &D |
| Time in the format specified by Regional Settings in Control Panel | &t |
| Time in 24-hour format | &T |
| Current page number | &p |
| Total number of pages | &P |
| Centered text (following &b) | &b |
| Right-aligned text (following &b&b) | &b&b |
| A single ampersand (&) | && |

When you are ready to print, use the <Ctrl+P> key combination, or the **File**, **Print** menu command, to open the Print dialogue box shown below.

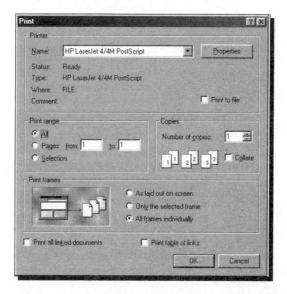

Make sure the correct printer is selected, choose the pages to be printed, how many copies you want, how you want any page frames to print, and finally click **OK** to start the printing process. You should be impressed with the results, we certainly were.

There are two very useful features in the above dialogue box, that we have not yet seen elsewhere:

- The **Print table of links** option, which when checked, gives a hard copy listing of the URL addresses of all the links present in the printed Web page.

- The **Print all linked documents** option, which not only prints the current Web page, but all those linked to it. This is a great way to print a whole Web site, as long as its links are not too deeply embedded.

## History Files

Explorer keeps track of all the Web pages and files you view, and stores temporary pointers to them in the **windows/history** folder. To return to them, click the History icon on the Toolbar which opens the History Explorer bar, as shown below. In this vertical bar, you can scroll off-line through the sites you have recently visited. Clicking on a blue Today, or Week of.., folder icon opens a list of the sites visited.

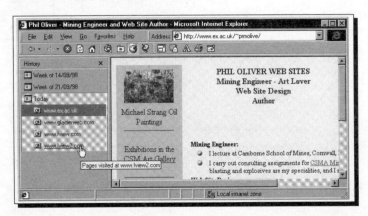

When you move the pointer over a yellow site folder icon in the list, the message 'Pages visited at..' is opened as shown on the previous page. Clicking a folder item, opens a further list of pages visited on that site and clicking a page item will reopen that Web page in the browser straight from the cache. Right-clicking on any list item gives you the options to **Open**, or to **Delete** it, as shown here.

You can control the length of time that Explorer keeps this History information in the settings sheet that is opened with the **View**, **Internet Options**, command.

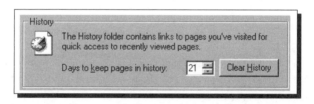

Ours was set for 21 days, as shown above, so all the saved History files expire 21 days after they are last visited. You can delete them immediately by clicking the **Clear History** button, to release the hard disc space used.

## The Cache:

You may have noticed that a Web page, especially one with lots of graphics, loads more quickly into Explorer if you have already recently viewed it. This is because all the pages and files you view are stored in a cache on your hard disc, which is in fact a system folder called 'Temporary Internet files', located in the Windows folder. The next time you access that page, depending on your settings, Explorer checks to see if the page has been updated before bringing it from the cache. If any change to the page has occurred, the new version is downloaded. If not, a cached copy is quickly retrieved. As with the History files, you control the cache, from the Options box which is opened with the **View**, **Internet Options** command.

The Temporary Internet files section of the General settings tabbed sheet is shown above. Pressing the **Delete Files** button will clear the cache, which will very rapidly free up space on your hard disc. The **Settings** button will open the following control box.

This shows that, in our case, these temporary files are stored in a cache in the C:\Windows\Temporary Internet Files folder, and that Web sites are checked for changes only the first time they are accessed in every Explorer session. To guarantee that you always view the most up to date version of Web pages, you may want to change this setting to check **Every visit to the page,** but page loading will be a little slower. You can also press the Refresh icon, or the <F5> key to refresh the current page being viewed. If there is a newer version of the page on its server this will then be downloaded to your PC.

If you are short of space on your hard disc, you can reduce the size of your cache by lowering the **Amount of disk space to use** slider. Again this will reduce the number of sites that can be cached, and may slow you down. If you have another hard disc you could also move the cache onto it by clicking the **Move Folder** button. The **View Files** option lets you look in the cache, but the only operation you can perform there is to open and view the contained files; even that option has a warning message though.

Any operations you carry out on the files in your cache, such as moving or deleting them, will affect any subscriptions you have activated in the **Favorites** sub-menu, as described in a later chapter.

## Security

Because of its design the Internet itself does not provide security for any data transmitted across it. As we saw in Chapter 1, data travelling between your computer and a server somewhere else in the world passes through a large number of computer systems. An operator at any one of these computers has the potential to view, manipulate, or even corrupt, your data, which can thus be very susceptible to fraud or other misuse by such unscrupulous individuals.

For most casual Web browsing this would not really matter, but if you are conducting business, or sending sensitive personal information, such as details of your credit card, you need security measures to make sure that your data is safe.

## Explorer Security Measures:

Netscape Communications originally developed a security technology called SSL, (short for Secure Sockets Layer protocol), which has become a standard since it was put into the public domain for the Internet community. This SSL protocol checks the identity of the server being accessed, carries out data encryption of any messages sent, and guarantees their general integrity. SSL is layered beneath the Internet application protocols (HTTP, Telnet, FTP, Gopher, etc.), but above the TCP/IP connection protocol. In this way it operates independently of the Internet protocols.

Microsoft Explorer supports SSL, as well as PCT (Private Communication Technology), which enables you to make secure credit-card purchases from a Web page. With these active on both your browser and the server you are transmitting to, your sensitive communications should be absolutely secure and unusable by third parties.

With Explorer you can tell whether a page, or document comes from a secure server by looking at the status bar. If a padlock icon is placed there when the page is opened, the site is secure.

## Security Zones:

To help protect your computer from downloading or running possibly harmful files, Explorer 4 divides your browsing world into zones, and allows you to assign sites to a zone with a suitable security level. You can tell which zone a current Web page is in by looking at the right side of the status bar, as shown here. Whenever you attempt to open or download content from the Web, Explorer checks the security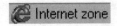

settings for that Web site's zone. There are four zones
and by default, pages downloaded from a Web site are
given the medium security settings associated with the
**Internet zone**.

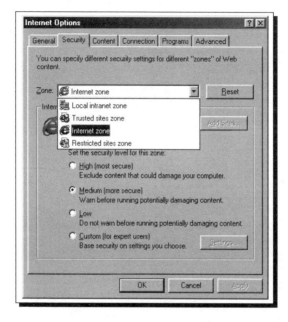

Security zones are controlled in the Security settings
sheet, shown above, which is opened with the **View**,
**Internet Options** command. If you are worried about
your system being 'contaminated' from a Web site,
click the **Add Sites** button here and give the site a
**Restricted Zone** rating.

## A Secure Transaction:

As an example of a typical secure transaction carried
out with Explorer version 4.1, we will step through the
process of ordering our copy of the shareware program
LView Pro which we downloaded earlier in the chapter.

From the LView Pro home page, shown on page 48, clicking the *... purchase...* link shown here, opens a

Security Alert box which warns you that you are about to enter a secure page. You have the option to disable this warning for the future, to get **More Info** or to continue by clicking **OK**.

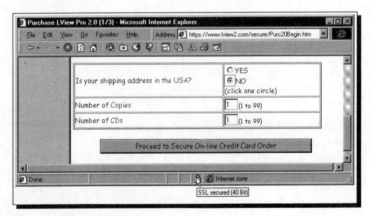

The above part page shows the padlock icon displayed in the status bar, indicating the Web page is secure. When you move the pointer over the padlock icon the level of site security is flagged as also shown above. By right-clicking the icon you can open a copy of the actual security certificate properties.

## The Microsoft Wallet

While we are on the subject of secure transactions, Explorer 4 has another new feature you may want to use if you do any Internet shopping. This is the Wallet which is accessed from the Content settings sheet opened with the **View**, **Internet Options**, command.

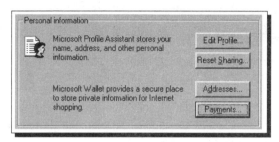

The first three buttons in the Personal Information section, shown above, let you enter a complete personal profile. The **Payments** button opens the Wallet, shown below, where you can **Add** details of your credit cards and attach passwords to allow their use. The facility is there, it's up to you whether you feel comfortable using it. Eventually I expect we all will.

## Different File Formats

While exploring the Web, you will encounter many different types of files and file formats. The way to tell the format of a file, and hence find out what it does, is to look at its extension, which is usually expressed as a dot followed by 2 to 4 letters. DOS and Windows 3.1 file extensions were limited to three characters, so a file extension with four letters is usually a Macintosh or UNIX file format.

Most of the files you encounter on the Web will be either text, graphics, audio or video files; some may be compressed. Some of the most common files to be found are:

**Compressed**    With extensions like .ZIP, .SIT and .TAR.

**Graphics**    With the extensions .JPEG (or .JPG), a popular compression file standard for photograph quality images; and .GIF, an older format developed by CompuServe in the late 1980s.

**Video**    With the popular extensions of .AVI, .MPG, .MOV, .QT.

**Sound**    Files come in .AIFF (for the Mac). .AU for the Mac and UNIX. .WAV for the PC, and .RA (Real Audio) a new proprietary system for delivering and playing real-time audio on the Web.

You may need to be able to identify these and other file types before you can use them, so we have included an Appendix of the main file formats at the back of this book.

# 5. WHERE SHALL WE GO TODAY?

For anyone not involved with the Web, Microsoft's advertising catch phrase "Where do you want to go today?" is probably a bit confusing. For those that do a little surfing the confusion is, how do we choose where to go?

You can literally spend hours following links from one place to another, and at the end of the day sometimes getting nowhere useful. But if you want some specific information you will have to use one, or more, of the many search engines that are available.

## Finding the Search Tools

There are a number of search tools, or engines, available to help you find what you want on the Web. Some search all the contents of documents, others only the file name. Most of them rank the search results in order depending on the number of times the searched-for words appear in a document, or on some other criteria.

Basically there are two types:

- Directories, like **Yahoo**, depend on people to submit a short description to the directory with the URL for new sites, which are then reviewed. A search request to the directory then looks for matches only in the descriptions submitted.

- Search engines like **Alta Vista**, **Lycos** and **Infoseek** will find individual pages of a Web site that match your search, even if the site itself has nothing to do with what you are looking for.

Each search tool seems to use a different method of searching, so your search results may vary when you use different ones. Be patient as you may not always find what you're looking for very easily.

At the end of Chapter 2 we saw that the easy way to find a search tool is to click the **Search** Toolbar icon and open the Explorer Search Bar. Otherwise you can use the **Help**, **Microsoft on the Web**, **Search the Web** menu command sequence, which opens a page like that shown below, with access to many of the main Search tools that are available. But by no means all of them!

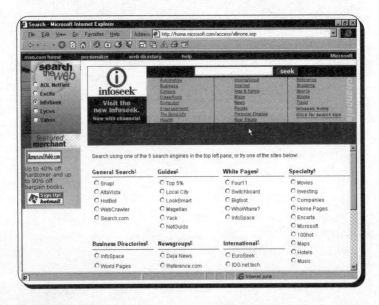

To the right of the search engine section are some tabulated search links which eventually lead to many sites which may well be of interest. Many of these are mostly relevant to the US, but not all, Europe and the UK are beginning to get more of a look-in these days.

Yahoo, one of the leading search tool operators, at the moment provides an Autosearch facility for Microsoft. You can carry out a rapid search by typing **go**, **find**, or **?**, followed by a space and then the word or phrase to search for, in the Address bar and then pressing the <Enter> key. This is a very quick way to get started on a search 'trail'.

## What is Available

In the next few pages we alphabetically list some of the main search tools that are available to you, with their URL addresses and a few comments on each. Be patient with them, they are all different. With most you simply type in the text you want to search for, but they usually offer much more complicated searches as well. If you have problems, look for a Help link and spend a few minutes reading how best to use the site's facilities. Don't forget that these are changing all the time, and no Web listing can ever be fully current!

### A2Z

```
http://a2z.lycos.com/
```

The Lycos A2Z directory starts with the most frequently linked sites, and adds concise, authoritative descriptions.

### ALTA VISTA

```
http://altavista.digital.com/
```

A product of Compaq, AltVista creates complete indexes of every word on every Web page or Usenet newsgroup it encounters, allowing you to make highly targeted searches. Alta Vista allows simple and advanced searches and can help you find your way through over 140 million Web pages.

### DEJANEWS

```
http://www.dejanews.com/
```

A specialist tool that searches Usenet newsgroups, and cuts through the millions of postings with absolute ease. We have provided an example of how DejaNews works at the end of the chapter.

### EXCITE

```
http://www.excite.com/
```

Offers two different ways to search: by keyword and by concept. Its concept-based searches allow you to search based on what you mean and not just what you say, by using plain English search 'phrases'. It places an icon next to each result allowing you to view more documents of a similar nature. Excite also allows you to view results in different modes.

## GAMELAN

http://www.gamelan.com/

A central repository for Java applications, sorted by category.

## G.O.D.

http://www.god.co.uk/

A European search tool using a unique global filter, or categorised site listings, it includes free online classified ads.

## HOTBOT

http://www.hotbot.com/

A search engine capable of indexing 10 million Web pages every day. HotBot's next generation interface is powered by the Inktomi search engine and lets you search on Java, VRML, and Netscape plug-ins, and allows you to limit searches by date, domain, or continent.

## INFOSEEK

http://www.infoseek.com/

Around since early 1995, Infoseek is well-known, well-reviewed and well-connected. In late 1996, a new service with 30 million URLs was introduced and listing a site took only minutes. Times have changed since May 1998 and it now takes up to 2 days.

## LYCOS

http://www.lycos.com/

Lycos is one of the oldest of the major search engines. It began as a project at Carnegie Mellon University. The name Lycos comes from the Latin for 'wolf spider'. Lycos operates for AOL NetFind in Europe. Lycos lists sites in two main ways. There are search engine listings, and there is an associated directory called 'Community Guides'.

## MAGELLAN

http://www.mckinley.com/

Developed by The McKinley Group, a publisher of print directories. Over 40,000 of the Web sites in its index have been reviewed and rated by their editorial staff. Magellan lets you navigate the Internet and preview content. You do a keyword search and are presented with a list of results each of which is described in a one paragraph summary and rated according to a four-star rating system. If you want to read a comprehensive review of the site, click on the Summary link. The number of stars tells you how good the site is, based on completeness of coverage, organisation, age, and ease of access.

## NORTHERN LIGHT

http://www.northernlight.com/
http://www.nlsearch.com/

Northern Light opened to general use in August 1997. While it doesn't have the strategic alliances of the other major search engines, it is seriously crawling significant portions of the web and thus qualifies to be among the major search engines. Northern Light features an ability to classify documents by topic, which it hopes will distinguish it from some of the other search services, even those with their own topical listings.

## STARTING POINT

http://www.stpt.com/

Use Starting Point to browse the Web, in categories such as news, business, sports, and entertainment.

## WEBCRAWLER

http://www.webcrawler.com/

This popular site offers a speedy Web search engine and a random-links feature to find new and unusual sites. WebCrawler searches the contents of pages within a site, for a match with the search terms you entered, even if the site itself is unrelated to what you are searching for. It also features a list of the 25 most visited sites on the Web.

## W3 SERVERS

http://www.w3.org/pub/DataSources/WWW/Servers.html

This directory at the World Wide Web Consortium lists registered Web servers around the world.

## WHAT'S NEW

http://www.emap.com/whatsnew/

A list of the best new sites on the Web, updated daily.

## WHOWHERE?

http://www.whowhere.com/

A comprehensive White Pages service for locating people and organisations on the Net. It intuitively handles misspelled or incomplete names, and it lets you search by initials.

## WORLD WIDE WEB WORM

http://wwww.cs.colorado.edu/wwww

Builds its index based on Web page titles and URL contents only. This is less inclusive, especially if poor page titles are used on a Web page.

## YAHOO

`http://www.yahoo.com/`

Probably the pioneer Internet guide, which has recently developed a special link with Microsoft. Yahoo is one of the most popular hierarchical indexes of Web sites by subject. You can search the index by subject, or specify a search term. Yahoo is good if you're searching for general information on a subject, but because of the way information is indexed, if you're looking for something specific, you probably won't get the best results with it. It is updated daily and gives up-to-the-minute sports scores, weather, headlines, and stock quotes - though mostly American of course.

If you can't find what you are looking for with one of these search tools then it may well not exist. Happy searching.

## DEJANEWS - As an Example

We cannot include examples of all the search tools listed, but to give you an idea of their power we have dabbled with a DEJANEWS search. For anyone starting to get to grips with the Usenet newsgroups this tool is essential.

As we saw earlier, the address of the Dejanews site is:
`http://www.dejanews.com/`

This opens the Web page shown on the next page, complete with colourful advertising, which seems to be a feature of most search pages now. I guess it helps keep the searches free to the rest of us.

This has a field for you to enter the text of a simple, **Search** of all the Usenet groups. The **power search** option lets you refine your search options further.

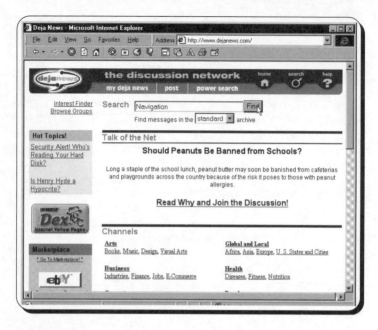

Clicking the **my deja news** link will open more details of the site and show you how to personalise them.

We are interested in sailing and generally finding our way round the oceans, so we entered **Navigation** in the **Search** box and then pressed **Find**. The first few of the 6,320 search results are shown below.

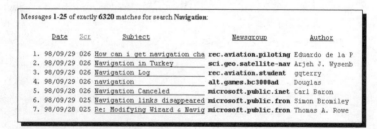

This was not really what we were looking for, but showed that 'navigation' was a popular word among the Usenet users. All of the underlined entries above are active links to news articles that have been posted.

We clicked the subject link for article 2 and read the posting, some of which is shown slightly amended below.

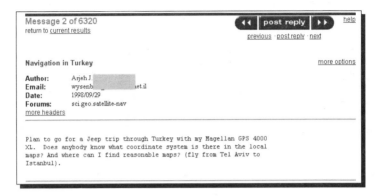

post reply    help
previous · post reply · next

Navigation in Turkey                                    more options

**Author:**   Arjeh J.
**Email:**    wysenb                    .et.il
**Date:**     1998/09/29
**Forums:**   sci.geo.satellite-nav
more headers

Plan to go for a Jeep trip through Turkey with my Magellan GPS 4000
XL. Does anybody know what coordinate system is there in the local
maps? And where can I find reasonable maps? (fly from Tel Aviv to
Istanbul).

Probably the content is not of much interest to many people in itself, but it's the principle we are trying to get over. At the top of the message area is a series of menu buttons and links which are worth looking at. The **more options** link opens the same message page, but with even more options for you to use, as shown on the left.

author profile
email reply
view thread
post new
subscribe
view for
bookmarking
text only

With the **previous** and **next** options you can work your way through the other messages in the retrieved listing and pressing **current results** will return you to the original full list. **view thread** will locate any other messages in the same series, so that you can follow the whole 'conversation'.

The **post reply** and **post new** options let you actually compose and send your own messages to the Usenet group, and **email reply** lets you send a personal message to the author, all without even leaving Dejanews. The **subscribe** option lets you register with Deja News, and **view for bookmarking** changes the view of the current message page to a unique message suitable to use as a Favorite.

71

Clicking **author profile** opens a page showing details of every message the writer of the current article has sent to the Usenet groups, as shown in the slightly 'censored' example below. This may help you assess the value of an article by showing you the writer's Usenet history.

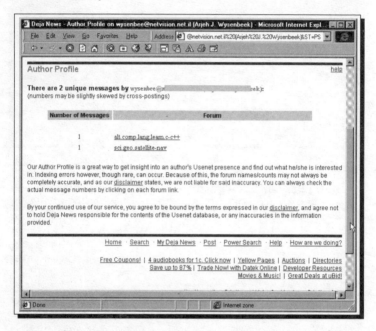

You can also use Dejanews to open, read and communicate with, your regular newsgroups. A useful facility, if you have problems with the Explorer Newsreader. In all, a very powerful facility, which is free of charge. Let's hope it stays that way.

# 6. FAVORITES AND CHANNELS

Using Favorites, which are Microsoft's version of Bookmarks (their spelling not ours!) is an easy way to access the Web pages that you need to visit on a regular basis. It is much easier to select a page URL address from a sorted list, than to look it up and manually type it into the Address field.

## Favorites

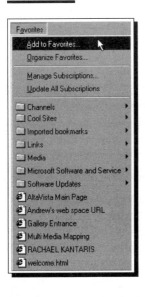

With Internet Explorer, a Favorite is simply a Windows 95 or Windows 98 shortcut to a Web page that the program places in the **windows\ favorites** folder.

When you first use Explorer there are some Favorites already available sorted into folders as shown here. Later, as your list of regular sites grows, your Favorites menu structure will grow too. In our example we have added the last six on the list. As we shall see it is very easy to then sort your own Favorites as well.

## Adding a Favorite:

There are several ways to add a Favorite to the menu. When you are viewing a Web page that you want to visit again, the easiest method is to right-click on the page and select **Add to Favorites** from the object menu. The **Favorites**, **Add to Favorites** menu command will also start the procedure. They both open the Add Favorite box shown on the next page.

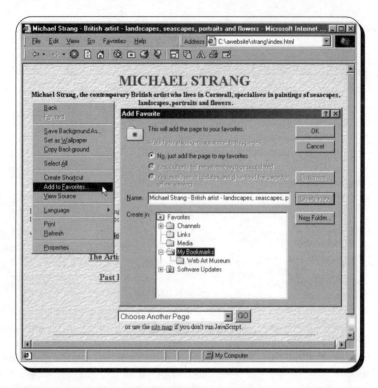

This composite shows several stages at once. We are adding the Michael Strang page to another of our lists using the right-click menu. Clicking the **Create in** button opens the lower part of the box, for you to select a folder to receive the new Favorite. Clicking the **OK** button then completes the process.

You could also simply click the first **OK** button to add the new Favorite to the bottom of the list. It would then appear at the bottom of the **Favorites** menu. The next time you open the **Favorites** menu that item should be there for you to use.  Each time you add a Web page like this, the page's title is offered as the name of the Favorite, but it is easy to  change this in the **Name** field above, or you can rename Favorites in the Organize Favorites window in the usual Windows 95/98 way.

## Using Favorites:

To open a Web page pointed to by a Favorite, you simply open the **F̲avorites** menu and click the item's name in the drop-down menu.

## The Organize Favorites Window

You won't have to visit many pages before your **F̲avorites** menu will get very full and difficult to use. It is then time to tidy up a little.

You choose the **F̲avorites**, **O̲rganize Favorites** command to open a window in which you can easily organise your Favorites, as shown below.

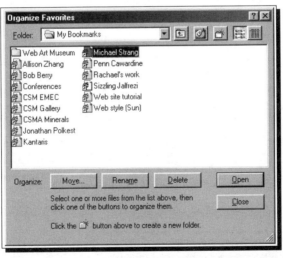

The window can contain both Favorite icons and folders to store them in, which can be nested in other folders to produce a hierarchical, or multilevel, menu. The window has its own menu buttons to manipulate and maintain your Favorites as you want. If you are happy handling files and folders in Windows 95/98 by dragging them around a window you will not need these buttons. You can do the same in this window.

## Selecting Items:

Double-clicking on a folder icon will display or hide its contents. Single-clicking on a Favorite icon, or folder, will select it, so that you can **Move**, **Delete**, or **Rename** it. Remember that actions carried out on a folder also affect the contents of that folder. If you delete a folder you will lose all its contents as well! But you do get the option to cancel. To select multiple items, you use the usual Windows convention of holding down the <Ctrl> key and clicking non-contiguous items, or the Shift key to select contiguous ones.

## Adding a New Folder:

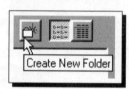

To add a new folder either, click the Create New Folder toolbar button, as shown here, or right-click in the empty window space and select **New**, **Folder** from the opened object menus. Both of these place a new folder at the end of the existing list box shown here. Type the new folder name and press the <Enter> key. You can then drag any of your existing Favorites into this folder, or nest folders by simply dragging one into another.

## Subscribing to a Web Page

Explorer 4 has a new way to help you keep up to date with your Web content. You can now 'subscribe' to your favourite Web sites and have Internet Explorer check them and automatically download new content, according to a schedule you specify. Don't worry, subscribing to a site is not like a magazine subscription, it does **not** require you paying fees at all. You can choose to either be notified that there is new content available, or have it downloaded to your hard disc at a convenient time, so you can view the pages off-line. This is an excellent new feature, which should save you a lot of actual connection time.

To subscribe to a new Web page, right-click on it in your browser window and select **Add to Favorites** from the object menu. As long as the page is not local, or located on your own hard disc, the Add Favorite box will offer you two choices for subscribing to the page.

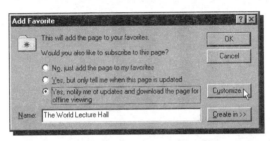

In our example above we have decided to 'go the whole hog' and make a full subscription, so to specify our downloading schedule we clicked the **Customize** button to start the Web Site Subscription wizard, shown next.

As you can see, this gives you the options to just **Download this page** or to **Download this page and pages linked to it**. Be careful with the latter as you can easily fill your hard disc overnight! Clicking the **Next** button moves to a box where you choose whether to have an e-mail sent to you when the site changes. Clicking **Next** again, opens the box below in which you choose whether to have the subscription updated automatically for you, or to do it yourself from the **Favorites** menu whenever you want to.

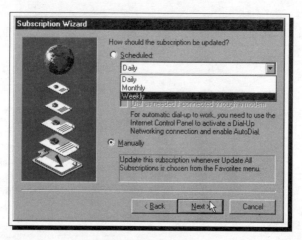

The last box in the Wizard lets you give the password details for sites that may need them. When this is done clicking the **Finish** button will complete the new subscription. In the future the Web page will be updated automatically at the frequency you set, as long as your computer is actually switched on at the time. A quick way to force a manual update at any time, is the **Update now** option on the right-click menu, shown here.

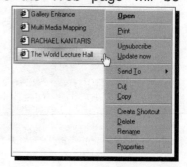

78

## Subscription Properties:

Every Subscribed Favorite has a set of properties which you can edit quite easily from its Properties box. The easiest way to open this box is to right-click on your Favorite and select **Properties** from the menu shown on the previous page.

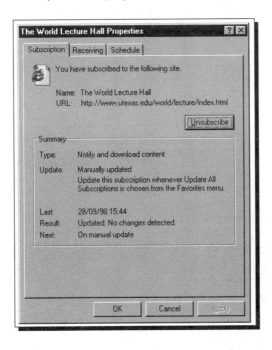

As shown above this set of Properties sheets gives you complete control of the subscription. We will leave it to you to explore the further possibilities here. The big advantage of subscriptions is that once a page, or pages, have been downloaded and saved on your computer, you can view them all without even being connected to the Internet, by using the **File**, **Work Offline** command. This not only saves your phone bill if you use a modem, but also means the pages load up almost instantly.

## Using Channels

**Channels**

A 'channel' is a feature new to Explorer 4 and is a Web site designed to deliver special content from the Internet to your computer, similar in a way to subscribing to a favourite Web site. With channels the content provider can suggest a schedule for your subscription, or you can customise one of your own. You can view channels in the browser, as a desktop item, or as your screen saver. To see what channels are available through the Microsoft Web site, click the Channels icon on the browser Toolbar, shown above.

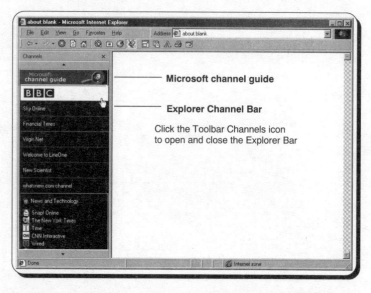

As shown above, this opens a list of sites in the Channel bar, which are updated frequently by the content providers. Some providers also give access to channels directly from their Web sites.

As you move your pointer over the Channel bar each channel title 'lights up' as it is activated. Clicking it will open the channel in the main browser window.

Maybe a better way to explore the enormous number of channels available is to open the Media Showcase window, shown below, by clicking the Microsoft channel guide, or the **Go**, **Channel Guide** command.

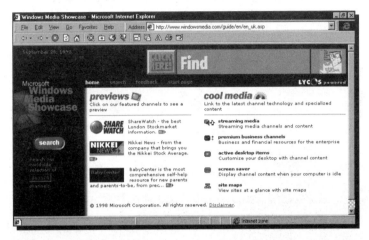

This page is updated all the time and will probably never look the same as that above. The **search** button gives the option of searching the 3,170 channels (available when we looked), but we clicked the **site maps** link and selected the ESI Share Channel from Page: 2. This opened the Channel Preview in the right window of the browser, part of which is shown below.

## Adding a Channel:

Clicking the **Visit Active Channel** button on the Preview page will let you get a flavour of what the site has to offer. If you like what you see, you can click the **Add Active Channel** button which opens a dialogue box similar to the Favorites box, as shown below.

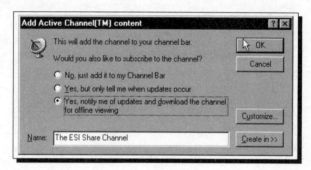

If you worked your way through the earlier part of this chapter, you should be quite happy with this box. We accepted the settings given and pressed the **OK** button, which opened another message window offering us a screen saver. We selected **Yes** but did not keep the Saver active very long, as

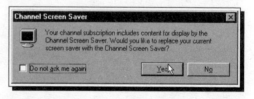

we also had work to do! Clicking the **Yes** button also started the process of downloading the files contained in the channel site.

When the downloading was completed our new channel was added to the Channel bar, as shown on the next page. When this was clicked, it showed the pages that had been added inside the channel, the second of which is open in our screen dump. A useful site if you need to buy or sell shares, or keep up to date with their prices, but you have to register.

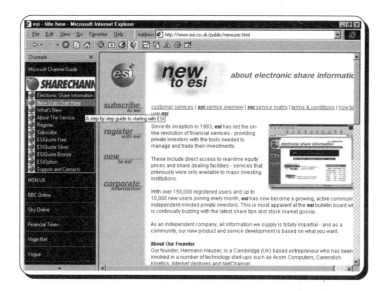

Adding channels is easy, the problem is deciding which ones you want. As another example below, the BBC channel lets you play live radio and video.

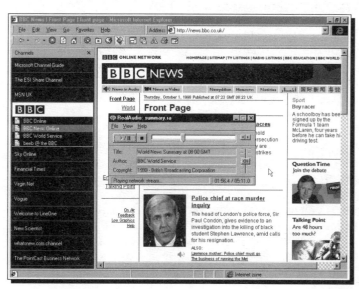

## Your Channel Bar:

You can organise the channels in your Channel bar in any way you want. The bar displays all of the channels installed on your computer, whether you subscribe to them or not. To delete a channel from the bar, right-click on it and choose **Delete** from the menu. In fact this menu, as shown here, lets you carry out most of the functions you can do on a channel.

If you want to change the order of channels in the bar, you simply drag them up, or down, the bar with either mouse button depressed. Releasing the button will reposition the channel.

## Desktop Shortcuts:

Another useful feature is that you can drag a channel from the bar to the desktop (with your right mouse button depressed) and create a shortcut to the channel there, as shown here.

Just clicking this icon on your desktop in the future will open the channel and the browser.

We found channels fascinating to play with, but unless you have a state of the art Pentium PC with hundreds of MB of RAM, and are permanently connected to the Internet, everything can very quickly grind to a halt. We also worry about the amount of data transmission required for them and the excessive bandwidths used. At the end of the day, somebody has to pay for all this, and we have a suspicion that it may well be all of us 'users', and in the not too distant future!

## The Active Desktop

The Active Desktop interface lets you put 'active content' from Web pages, or from a channel, on your desktop. This is a feature to use with care, as

discussed on the last page, but it can be usefully employed. For example, we have used the active item from the BBC shown here. In our experience, though, many active items create system errors when they are left active for any length of time.

If you are running Windows 95 or Windows NT 4.0, to use the Active Desktop you must have the new desktop installed, but it is already part of Windows 98.

### Installing the New Desktop:

If you did not install the new desktop when you installed the Explorer 4 browser you will have to do it now, if you want to use its facilities. If you have the program on a CD-ROM simply go back to Chapter 2 and repeat the installation making sure you install the Windows Desktop Update. Otherwise open the **Start** menu, point to **Settings**, click **Control Panel** and then double-click the Add/Remove Programs icon. Click Microsoft Internet Explorer 4.0, followed by **Add/Remove** and then select **Add Windows Desktop Update from Web site**. According to Microsoft, if you don't see this option, then the new desktop is already installed.

To turn on the Active Desktop right-click the desktop, point to the **Active Desktop** option and make sure **View as Web Page** is selected.

## Active Desktop Settings:

You can control all of the settings for your desktop in the Display Properties box, which is opened by right-clicking on the desktop and selecting **Properties**.

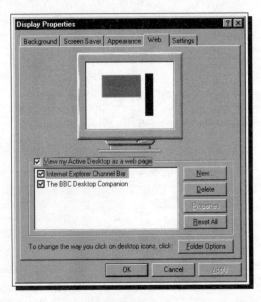

The Active Desktop settings are in the Web tabbed sheet of this box, as shown above. Any active items installed on your system will be listed here. When they are selected, a tick is placed alongside them, and they will be active when you close the dialogue box. The desktop will not be active unless the **View my Active Desktop as a web page** option is selected.

You can **Delete** items here as well as adding **New** ones, but the easiest way to add new active items from a Web site is to right-click a link on a Web page, drag it to the desktop, and then click **Create Active Desktop item(s) Here**.

## Active Desktop Problems:

If your Active Desktop turns black the next time you use it, it is because Explorer has added its own wallpaper, which of course is black. No panic, open the Background tab sheet in the Display Properties box and set the Wallpaper to **None**, unless you like being in the dark!

While we are on the subject of problems, we have twice been presented with the message below.

---

# Active Desktop Recovery

Internet Explorer has experienced a problem or error. As a precaution, your Active Desktop has temporarily been turned off. To start the Active Desktop again, use the following troubleshooting tips:

- Did your browser stop working or did you restart your computer without shutting down? If so, click <u>Restore my Active Desktop</u>.

- Did you recently add a new item to your Active Desktop? If so, try the following:

  1. Click on the **Start** button, point to **Settings**, point to **Active Desktop**, and then click **Customize my Desktop**.
  2. Clear the check box for the item you added most recently.

- Do you want to turn off your Active Desktop and restore your wallpaper? If so, click the **Start** button, point to **Settings**, point to **Active Desktop**, then click **View as Webpage** to remove the check mark.

---

This is all self-explanatory, but the Active desktop feature is not particularly robust, especially in an upgraded Windows 95 environment. So far we have not had too many problems with Windows 98, though.

# 7. E-MAIL WITH OUTLOOK EXPRESS

Internet Explorer 4 comes with the very powerful mail and news facility, Outlook Express, built into it, which makes it very easy for you to send and receive e-mail messages. We are impressed with Outlook Express and use it for our e-mail correspondence.

## What is E-mail

E-mail, or electronic mail, is cheaper, quicker, and usually much easier to prepare and send than Post Office mail. So what is an e-mail? It's simply an electronic message sent between computers which can include attachments like pictures, document files or Web pages. The message is passed from one computer to another as it travels through the Internet, with each computer reading its e-mail address and routing it further until it reaches its destination, where it is stored in a 'mailbox'. This usually only takes a few minutes, and sometimes only seconds.

You can use e-mail for keeping in touch with friends and family and for professional reasons. You can send e-mail to most people, anywhere in the world, as long as they have their own e-mail address. These days all Internet service providers offer an e-mail address and mailbox facility to all their customers.

To retrieve your e-mail messages you have to contact your mailbox, download them to your PC, and then read and process them (just like any other mail). As we shall see, Outlook Express makes this whole procedure very easy and takes most of the mystery out of the whole e-mail process.

## E-mail Addresses:

An e-mail address usually has two main parts, which are separated with the '@' character, and usually contain at least one dot (the '.' character). The following is a typical, if short, example.

**aperson@organisation.co.uk**

The part before the @ is the user name which identifies him, or her, at the mailbox. This user name is usually made up from the name and initials of the user.

After the @ comes the domain name, which identifies the computer where the person has a mailbox and is usually the name of a company, a university, or other organisation. There is a central register of these domain names, as each must be unique. When you set up your account, you can sometimes get your service provider to customise a domain name for you, at a price, of course. Otherwise you will probably use the domain name of the service provider itself.

Next, there's a '.' or dot, followed by two, or three, letters that indicate the type of domain it is. In our example above this is **.co** which means the host is a business or commercial enterprise, located in the United Kingdom (**.uk**). In the USA this would be **.com** instead, but not followed by a country identifier.

A host name ending with **.edu** means the host is a US university or educational facility. A UK university would be **.ac.uk**. A **.org** indicates the host is a US non-commercial organisation.

Some of the more common extensions you might encounter are:

| | |
|---|---|
| **edu** | Educational sites in the US |
| **com** | Commercial sites in the US |
| **gov** | Government sites in the US |
| **net** | Network administrative organisations |
| **mil** | Military sites in the US |

| | |
|---|---|
| **org** | Organisations in the US that don't fit into other categories |
| **fr** | France |
| **ca** | Canada |
| **uk** | United Kingdom |
| **\*\*** | Other county codes |

Once you get used to these address parts, they begin to make more sense. For example, the writer's e-mail address is

**prmolive@csm.ex.ac.uk**

This reads quite easily as:

PRM Oliver located at Camborne School of Mines, part of the University of Exeter, which is an academic institution in the UK.

So if you know where somebody works you can even make an attempt to guess his, or her, e-mail address. A home address obtained through a commercial Internet provider would not be very easy though.

## Finding an E-mail Address:

**White Pages**[3]

○ Four11
○ Switchboard
○ Bigfoot
○ WhoWhere?
○ InfoSpace

The **Help**, **Microsoft on the Web**, **Search the Web** menu command sequence in Microsoft Explorer, opens a Search page which gives easy access to several e-mail address directory sites, as shown here. It is easy to use one of these to search for someone's e-mail address, as these directories are getting more detailed all the time.

## Using Outlook Express

Outlook
Express

To start the Outlook Express program, click the Desktop icon shown here, or the small icon on the left of the Taskbar. In either case the window shown below should be opened.

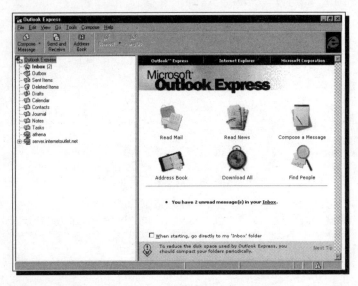

Before you can use your browser to send, or receive, mail you have to tell the program how to connect to your server's facilities. You do this by completing your personal e-mail connection details in the Internet Connection Wizard shown on the next page, which opens when you first attempt to use the Read Mail facility above.

The other way to enter this Wizard, if it does not open, or you want to change your connection details, is to use the **Tools**, **Accounts** menu command, select the mail tab and click **Add**, followed by **Mail**.

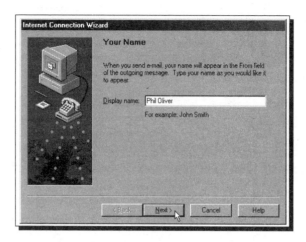

You type your name in the first box, as shown above, your e-mail address in the second, and your e-mail server details in the third, as shown for us, below.

To complete some of the details here you may need to ask your Internet service provider, or system administrator, for help. The ones shown here will obviously only work for the writer, so don't try them! If you need more information try clicking the **Help** button; it is quite informative.

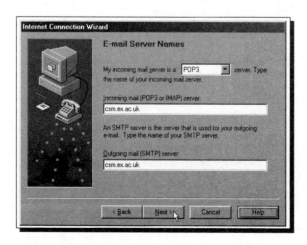

In the next box enter your log-in name and password. Details of these should have been given to you by your Internet service provider or system administrator when you opened your 'service account'. You are then asked to provide a 'friendly' name to identify this account. This is needed because you can have several accounts in the program at the same time. Yet another box lets you choose the type of connection you have, the options being LAN (local area network), a phone line or a software dialler. You have now completed the Wizard so press **Finish** to return you to the Internet Accounts box, with your new account set up as shown below.

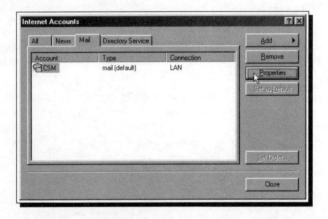

In the future, selecting the account in this box and clicking the **Properties** button will give you access to the settings sheets to check, or change, your details.

Read Mail

Once your connection is established, you can click the Read Mail icon, shown here, or the **Inbox** entry in the Folder List on the left side of the Outlook Express opening window. Both of these actions open the Inbox, which the first time opened, will probably contain some messages from Microsoft, as shown on the facing page.

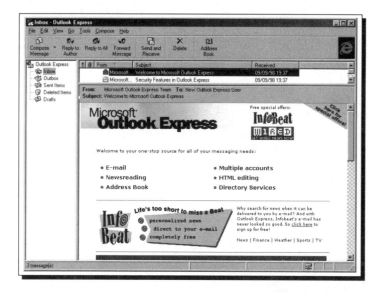

These messages are well worth reading as they demonstrate some of the features of Outlook Express and show how decorative your e-mails can be.

The illustration above shows the default Outlook Express Main window layout, which consists of a Folder List to the left, a Message List to the right and a Preview Pane below it. The Folder List contains all the active mail folders, news servers and newsgroups. Clicking on one of these places its contents in the Message List, and clicking on a message opens a Preview of it below for you to see. Double-clicking on a message opens the message in its own window.

To check your mail, click the **Send and Receive** Toolbar icon which will download any new messages from your mailbox to your hard disc. You can then read and process your mail at your leisure without necessarily being still connected to the Internet.

With the default set-up, Outlook Express will only check your mailbox when you click the **Send and Receive** icon. We suggest you make a change in the **Tools**, **Options**, **General** tab settings sheet. Selecting the **Check for new messages every** 10 **minute(s)** option will make the program check your mail box when it starts and at regular intervals while it is open.

## A Trial Run

Before explaining in more detail the features of Outlook Express we will step through the procedure of sending a very simple e-mail message. The best way to test out any unfamiliar e-mail features is to send a test message to your own e-mail address. This saves wasting somebody else's time, and the message can be very quickly checked to see the results.

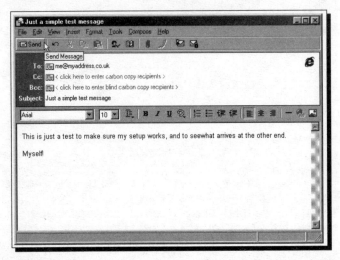

Click the **Compose Message** Toolbar icon to open the New Message window, shown above. Type your own e-mail address in the **To:** field, and a title for the message in the **Subject:** field. The text in this subject field will form a header for the message when it is received, so it helps to show in a few words what the message is about. Type your message and when you are happy with it, click the **Send** toolbar icon, which is pointed to above.

The box shown here may then display to explain what has happened to your message. By default, it is stored in an Outbox folder, and pressing the **Send and Receive** Toolbar icon will send it, hopefully straight into your mailbox. When Outlook Express next checks for mail, it will find the message and download it into the Inbox folder, as shown below, for you to read and enjoy!

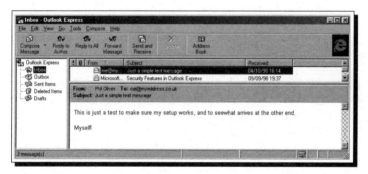

After the initial opening window (see page 92), Outlook Express uses three other main windows, which we will refer to as; the Main window which opens next, the Read Message window for reading your mail; and the New Message window, to compose your outgoing mail messages.

## The Main Window

The Main window consists of a Toolbar, a menu, and three panes with the default display shown in our example on page 95. You can choose different pane layouts, and customise the Toolbar, with the **View**,

**Layout** menu command, but we will let you try these for yourself.

## The Folders List:

The folders pane contains a list of your mail folders, and as we shall see later, your news servers and newsgroups. There are always at least four mail folders, as shown, but you can add your own with the **File**, **Folder**, **New Folder** menu command from the Main window. You can delete them again with the **File**, **Folder**, **Delete** command. These operations can also be carried out after right-clicking a folder in the list.

## The Message List:

When you select a folder, by clicking it in the Folders list, the Message list shows the contents of that folder. Brief details of each message are displayed on one line, as shown on the previous page.

The first column shows the message priority, if any, and the second shows whether the message has an

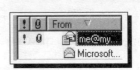

attachment. Both of these are indicated by icons on the message line, like our example to the left. The 'From' column shows the message status icon (listed on the next page) and the name of the sender; 'Subject' shows the title of each mail message, and 'Received' shows the date it reached you. You can control what columns display in this pane with the **View**, **Columns** menu command.

To sort a list of messages, you can click the mouse pointer in the title of the column you want the list sorted on, clicking it again will sort it in reverse order. The sorted column is shown with a triangle mark, as can be seen above. If you want to keep a message when you have read it, you can simply drag it to one of the folders in the Folder List.

| This icon | Indicates this |
|---|---|
| 🖇 | The message has one or more files attached. |
| ⬆ | The message has been marked high priority by the sender. |
| ⬇ | The message has been marked low priority by the sender. |
| ⊠ | The message has been read. The message heading appears in light type. |
| ✉ | The message has not been read. The heading appears in bold type. |
| 📝 | The message is in progress in the Draft folder. |
| ✉ | The message is digitally signed and unopened. |
| ✉ | The message is encrypted and unopened. |
| ✉ | The message is digitally signed, encrypted and unopened. |
| ✉ | The message is digitally signed and has been opened. |
| ✉ | The message is encrypted and has been opened. |
| ✉ | The message is digitally signed and encrypted, and has been opened. |
| ✉ | The unread message has something wrong with the digital signature. |
| ✉ | The unread message has something wrong with the encryption. |
| ✉ | The unread message has something wrong with the encryption and digital signature. |
| ✉ | The opened message has something wrong with the digital signature. |
| ✉ | The opened message has something wrong with the encryption. |
| ✉ | The opened message has something wrong with the digital signature and encryption. |
| ⊞ | The message has responses that are collapsed. Click the icon to show all the responses (expand the thread). |
| ⊟ | The message and all of its responses are expanded. Click the icon to hide all the responses (collapse the thread). |
| ☑ | The unread message header is on an IMAP server. |
| ☑ | The opened message is marked for deletion on an IMAP server. |

## The Preview Pane:

When you select a message in the Message list, by clicking it once, it is displayed in the Preview pane, which takes up the rest of the window. This lets you read the first few lines to see if the message is worth bothering with. If so, double clicking the header, in the Message list, will open the message in the Read Message window, as shown later in the chapter.

You could use the Preview pane to read all your mail, especially if your messages are all on the short side, but it is easier to process them from the Read Message window.

## The Main Window Toolbar:

Opens the New Message window for creating a new mail message, with the To: field blank.

Opens the New Message window for replying to the current mail message, with the To: field pre-addressed to the original sender. The original Subject field is prefixed with Re:.

Opens the New Message window for replying to the current mail message, with the To: field pre-addressed to all that received copies of the original message. The original Subject field is prefixed with Re:.

Opens the New Message window for forwarding the current mail message. The To: field is blank. The original Subject field is prefixed with Fw:.

Connects to the mailbox server and downloads waiting messages, which it places in the Inbox folder. Sends any messages waiting in the Outbox folder.

Deletes the currently selected message and places it in the Deleted Items folder.

Opens the Address Book.

## The Read Message Window

If you double-click a message in the Message list of the Main window the Read Message window is opened, as shown below.

This is the best window to read your mail in. It has its own menu system and Toolbar, which lets you rapidly process and move between the messages in a folder.

## The Read Message Toolbar:

**Save this message** - Opens the Save Message As box for you to save the message to a disc file. The possible disc formats being, .txt for an ASCII text file, .eml for a Mail file and .htm for a Web page file.

**Print** - Sends the message to the current printer using all the default print settings.

**Copy** - Copies selected text to the Windows clipboard.

**Delete** - Deletes the current message, places it in the Deleted Items folder, and closes the Read Message window.

 **Reply to Author** - Opens the New Message window for replying to the current mail message, with the To: field pre-addressed to the original sender.

 **Reply All** - Opens the New Message window for replying to the current mail message, with the To: field pre-addressed to all that received message copies.

 **Forward** - Opens the New Message window for forwarding the current mail message. The To: field is blank. The original Subject field is prefixed with Fw:.

 **Previous** - Displays the previous mail message in the Read Message window. The button appears depressed if there are no previous messages.

 **Next** - Displays the next mail message in the Read Message window. The button appears depressed if there are no more messages.

 **Address Book** - Opens the Address Book window for you to add the details of the message sender.

The other two icons on this Toolbar, **Digitally sign message** and **Encrypt message**, seem to be permanently 'greyed out'.

## Viewing File Attachments:

Until fairly recently, e-mail on the Internet was good only for short text notes. You couldn't send attachments like formatted document or graphic files with your messages. That has now changed with the advent of MIME, which stands for Multipurpose Internet Mail Extension. With the Outlook Express you can send Web pages, other formatted documents, photos, sound and video files as attachments to your main e-mail message, and some of them as part of the actual message itself.

One thing to be careful of though, is to make sure that the person you are sending your message to has e-mail software capable of decoding them. In our experience most people seem to stick to their tried and trusted 'old' software that does not.

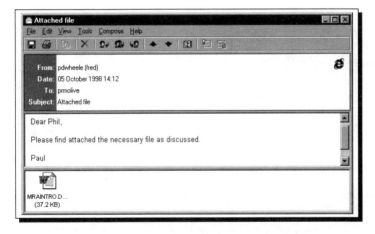

A file attachment appears at the bottom of the message in the Read Message window as shown above. To view, or run the file, double-click its icon. To save a file attachment, use the **File**, **Save Attachments** menu command, or right-click the attachment and select the **Save As** option.

To display, or run, an attachment from the preview pane, click the paper clip file attachment icon in the preview pane header, and then click the file name. To save it from the preview pane, hold down the <Ctrl> key when you click the displayed file name.

## The New Message Window

We briefly looked into the New Message window earlier in the chapter. This is the window, shown below, that you will use to create any messages you want to send electronically from Outlook Express. It is important to understand its features, so that you can get the most out of it.

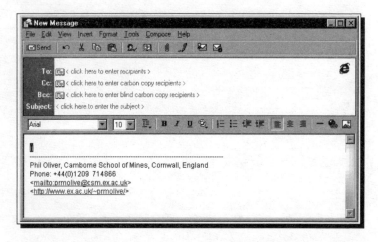

As we saw, this window can be opened by using the **Compose Message** Toolbar icon from the Main window, as well as the **Compose**, **New Message** menu command from any window, or the <Ctrl+N> keyboard shortcut.

It has its own menu system and Toolbar, which let you rapidly prepare and send your new e-mail messages.

## Your Own Signature :

If you have created a signature from the Main window in the **Tools**, **Stationery**, **Signature** box, as shown below, its text is placed at the end of the message creation area.

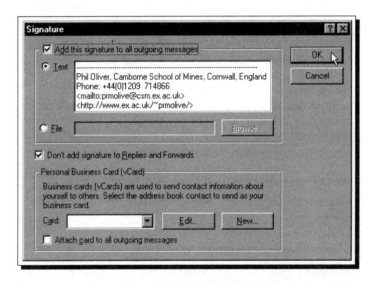

You could also create a more fancy signature file in a text editor like Notepad, or WordPad, including the text and characters you want added to all your messages, and point to it in the **File** section of this box. We have chosen to **Add this signature to all outgoing messages**, but you could leave this option blank and use the **Signature** Toolbar icon if you prefer.

You now have the option to use electronic business cards and attach them to your messages. To use this facility you must first create the 'vCard' in the Address Book, by clicking the **New** button.

## Message Stationery:

Another feature new to Outlook Express lets you send special messages on pre-formatted stationery for added effect, as in our example below.

To access these, use the **Compose**, **New Message using** command from the Main window and either select from the **1** to **10** list of last used formats, or open the box below with the **More Stationery** command.

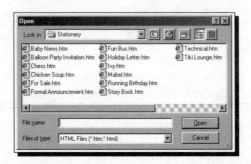

## The New Message Toolbar:

 **Send Message** - Sends the created message, either to the recipient, or to the Outbox folder.

 **Undo** - Undoes the last editing action.

 **Cut** - Cuts selected text to the Windows clipboard.

 **Copy** - Copies selected text to the Windows clipboard.

 **Paste** - Pastes the contents of the Windows clipboard into the current message, at the insertion point.

 **Check Names** - Checks that names match your entries in the address book, or are in the correct e-mail address format (name@company).

 **Select Recipients** - Opens the Select Recipients box for you to rapidly select who should receive copies of the message.

 **Insert file** - Opens the Insert Attachment window for you to select a file to be attached to the current message.

 **Insert signature** - Adds your signature to the bottom of the message, as long as you have specified one in the **Tools**, **Options**, **Signature** box.

**Digitally sign message** - Add a digital signature to the message to confirm to the recipient that it is from you.

 **Encrypt message** - Encode the message so that only the recipient will be able to read it.

## Message Formatting:

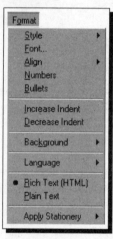

Outlook Express provides quite sophisticated formatting options for an e-mail editor from the **Format** menu and Toolbar, as shown below. These only work if you prepare the message in HTML format, as used in Web documents.

In the **Tools**, **Options**, **Send** box you can set this to be your default mail sending format. To use the format for the current message only, select **Rich Text (HTML)** from the **Format** menu, as we have done here.

With HTML, the above Format Toolbar is added to the New Message window and all the **Format** menu options are then made active. The **Style** command lets you choose an HTML formatting style, **Font** gives you full control of the message font type, and its size and attributes. These functions are also provided by the first seven Format Toolbar buttons.

The **Align** command, and the three Toolbar buttons, let you format your message paragraphs with **Left**, **Center** or **Right** alignment. **Numbers** and **Bullets**, give you indented numbered or bulleted paragraph styles, suitable for lists. The two **Indent** commands let you increase or decrease paragraph indents; **Background** lets you choose between a picture or a colour background for your message; **Language** gives a choice of other languages to use (this can be useful if your message contains accents or foreign letters. The **Plain Text** option disables the use of HTML and your message will then consist of plain unformatted text, and you will not then be able to **Apply Stationery**.

Most of these formatting features are quite well demonstrated in Microsoft's opening message to you. You should be able to prepare some very easily readable e-mail messages with these features, but remember that not everyone will be able to read the work you spent hours creating. It is sometimes better to stick to plain text, not only can everyone read it, but it is much quicker to use.

## Setting Message Priority:

Outgoing e-mail messages can be given one of three priority ratings, so that their recipients can rank their mail in order of importance. This is only of any real use, though, if the person receiving the message can use the facility.

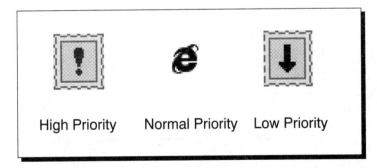

High Priority    Normal Priority    Low Priority

To set message priorities use the **Tools**, **Set Priority** command in the New Message window and choose between **High**, **Normal** (the default), or **Low**. These change the stamp icon on the message being created as shown at the bottom of the previous page.

## Adding Attachments:

If you want to send a Web page, or other type of file as an attachment to your main e-mail message you simply click the **Insert file** Toolbar button and select the file to attach. This opens the Insert Attachment dialogue box, for you to select the file, or files, you want to go with your message.

The attached files are 'placed' in a special section at the bottom of your message, as shown below. Right-clicking in this section gives you two choices, to **Add** further attached files, or to change the icon **View** settings in the section. Double-clicking an icon here will open the file in its application, for you to check, or edit, before it is sent.

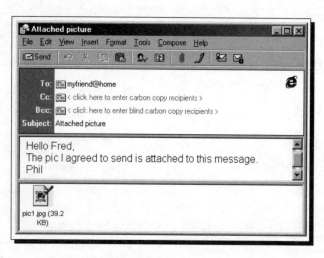

## Sending E-mail Messages

When you have filled in the address fields, typed and formatted the body of your message, added any attachments, and maybe placed a signature, you simply click the **Send Message** Toolbar icon, shown here, to start the transmission process. What happens to the message next depends on your settings.

If you want to keep the message and send it later, maybe with several others to save on your telephone bill, make sure the **Send messages immediately** option is not selected in the **Tools**, **Options**, **Send** settings box. In this case, clicking the above **Send Message** Toolbar icon places the message in the Outbox folder.

When you are ready to send your held messages you click the **Send and Receive** Toolbar icon on the Main window. If you forget to do this, Outlook Express will prompt you with a message box when you attempt to exit the program.

When the **Send messages immediately** option is selected, your messages will be sent on their way as soon as you click the **Send Message** Toolbar button. This option is best used if you have a permanent connection to the Internet, or your e-mail is being sent over an internal network, or Intranet.

## Replying to a Message

When you receive an e-mail message that you want to reply to, Outlook Express makes it very easy to do. The reply address and the new message subject fields are both added automatically for you. Also, by default, the original message is quoted in the reply window for you to edit as required.

With the message you want to reply to open, either click the **Reply to Author** Toolbar icon, use the **Compose**, **Reply to Author** menu command, or use the <Ctrl+R> keyboard shortcut. All these actions open the New Message window and the message you are replying to will, by default, be placed under the insertion point.

You should not, however, leave all of the original message in your reply. This can be bad practice, which can rapidly make new messages very large and time consuming to download. You should usually edit the quoted text, so that it is obvious what you are referring to. One or two lines may even be enough.

## Removing Deleted Messages

Whenever you delete a message it is actually moved to the Deleted Items folder. If ignored, this folder gets bigger and bigger over time, so you need to check it

 every few days and manually re-delete messages you are sure you will not need again. In which case you are given this last warning message.

If you are confident that you will not need this safety net, you can opt to **Empty messages from the 'Deleted Items' folder on exit** in the **Tools**, **Options**, **General** settings box, opened from the Main window. You will then have a short time to change your mind before they are finally deleted.

## The Address Book

E-mail addresses are often quite complicated and not easy to remember at all. With Outlook Express there is a very useful Address Book built in and an almost empty example of one is shown here.

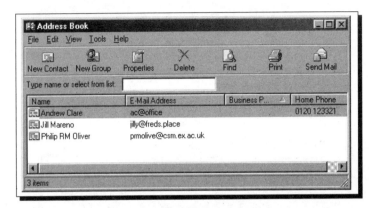

It can be opened from the Main window with the **Tools**, **Address Book** menu command, or the **Address Book** Toolbar icon. To open it in a New Message window, click the **Select** Recipients icon, or any of the To, Cc, or Bcc icons.

You can manually add a person's full details and e-mail address, in the Properties box that opens when you click the **New Contact** Toolbar icon. The **New Group** icon lets you create a grouping of e-mail addresses, you can then send mail to everyone in the group with one operation.

We will leave it to you to find your way round this very comprehensive facility. Don't forget that it has its own Help system that you can use.

To send a new message to anyone listed in your Address Book, open a New Message window and click the **Select Recipients** Toolbar icon.

In this window you can select a person's name and click either the **To:->** button to place it in the **To:** field of your message, the **Cc->** button to place it in the **Cc:** field, or the **Bcc->**button to place it in the **Bcc:** field.

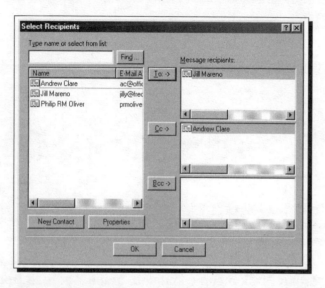

The **New Contact** button lets you add details for a new person to the Address Book, and the **Properties** button lets you edit an existing entry.

## The Inbox Assistant

If you are ever in the situation of receiving e-mail messages from a source you do not want to hear from, you can use the Inbox Assistant to filter your incoming messages. Unwanted ones can be placed in your Deleted Items folder straight away. It is also useful for sorting incoming messages and automatically routing them to their correct folders.

To open the Assistant, which is shown on the facing page, use the **Tools**, **Inbox Assistant** menu command. Click the **Add** button and type the criteria you want the incoming message to match in the Properties box.

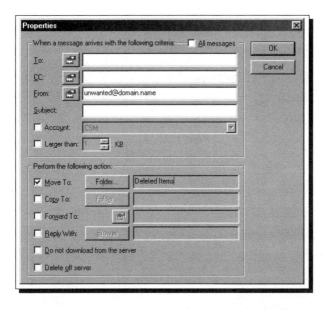

In our example above, we have set the Assistant to intercept any messages from the fictitious e-mail address 'unwanted@domain.name' and send them for immediate deletion.

You can set multiple rules for incoming messages and control the priority that messages are sorted in the list. The higher up a multiple list a condition is the higher will be its priority.

If an incoming message matches more than one rule, then it is sorted according to the first rule it matches in your list.

# Mailing Lists

When you start using e-mail you want to receive lots of messages, but until your friends get active there is often a lull. This is the time to join a mailing list.

Mailing lists are automatic mailing systems where a message sent to a list address is automatically sent on to all the other members of the list. The programs that manage this automatic mailing have names like Listserv, or Majordomo, which usually form part of the List address. Some of these lists are moderated and work much like journals, where submissions are accepted, sometimes edited, and then forwarded to subscribers. Others, however, have no constraints put on their contents! Although the quality and quantity vary from list to list, you can often find a wealth of free information in them.

To subscribe to a list, you need to know the name of the list and its address. Commands can vary between different lists, but they often follow the format given below. Note that there is a difference between the address to which you send postings, or messages, for the list, and the address you use for subscribing to it. Be sure to distinguish between these two addresses. One of the most common mistakes made by new Internet users is to send subscription requests to list addresses, which are then forwarded to all the members on the list. Please don't make this mistake, it can be annoying and time consuming for other list readers.


## List Subscription Commands:

All of these commands go to the subscription address:

**sub *listname First Last***   To subscribe to *listname*, with your *First* and *Last* names given.

| **signoff** *listname* | To unsubscribe from a list. |
| **set** *listname* **nomail** | To turn off mail from a list if you are going away. |
| **set** *listname* **mail** | To turn the mail back on when you return. |

## Finding a Suitable List:

There are literally thousands of Mailing lists which you can join, covering almost every subject imaginable, from science, to art, to hobbies, and even ones on kinky sex. One of the biggest problems is finding the ones which interest you.

Fortunately, there are several Web sites which give details of Mailing lists. A good one we have used, with lists grouped by topic should be found at:

**http://wwwneosoft.com/internet/paml/bysubj.html**

This will put you in direct contact with your selected lists, where you will get instructions on how to subscribe and proceed. Make sure you keep a copy of any instructions, you will need them in the future, if you want to unsubscribe, or change your subscription details.

Once you have mastered Mailing lists you need never have an empty mailbox again.

## Often Used E-mail Symbols

Once you start receiving messages from lists and other places around the globe, you may encounter some of the following acronyms, and symbols, which people often use to relieve the general boredom of life.

## Acronyms:

| | |
|---|---|
| BTW | By the way |
| CU | See you (bye) |
| FAQ | Frequently asked question |
| FYI | For your information |
| IMHO | In my humble opinion |
| IMO | In my opinion |
| ROTFL | Rolling on the floor laughing |
| RTFM | Read the manual! |
| TTYL | Talk to you later |

## Smileys:

You tilt your head sideways to see them:

| | |
|---|---|
| :-) | Smiling |
| :-D | Laughing |
| ;-) | Winking |
| :-O | Surprise |
| :-( | Frowning, Sad |
| :-I | Indifferent |
| :-/ | Perplexed |
| :-{) | Smiley with a moustache |
| 8-) | Smiley with glasses |
| <:-| | Dunce |
| :-X | My lips are sealed |
| :-> | Sarcastic |

If these appeal to you, you can get a more comprehensive selection from the *Unofficial Smiley Dictionary* reached at the following Web address:

**http://www.eff.org/papers/eegtti/eeg_286.html#SEC287**

# 8. NEWS WITH OUTLOOK EXPRESS

Discussion groups, or 'newsgroups', are a main feature of the Internet and are easily accessed with the Outlook Express. They are often known as Usenet groups and consist of over 35,000 separate news groups which let you actively take part in discussion on a vast number of topics. In fact almost any subject you could think of is covered, and the number of groups is growing larger all the time.

Outlook Express is a program you can use for viewing, and posting (or mailing), messages to these Usenet groups. Unlike e-mail, which is usually 'one-to-one', newsgroups could be said to be 'one-to-many'.

## How Usenet Works

Usenet messages are shipped around the world, from host system to host system, using one of several available protocols, that you don't need to bother too much about. Your host server stores all of its Usenet messages in one place, which everybody with an account on the system can access, if they want. That way, no matter how many people actually read a given message, each host has to store only one copy of it. The host systems contact each other regularly and bring themselves up to date with the latest Usenet messages, sometimes this happens thousands of times a day.

Usenet is huge. We have seen it quoted that every day Usenet users transmit over 60 million characters into the system. Some of this information has to be of use! In fact there are so many active groups now, it is unlikely that your server will handle them all. This can be frustrating, if you keep seeing references to a group that you cannot access through your server.

# Usenet Newsgroups

The basic building block of Usenet as we have seen is the newsgroup, which is a collection of messages with a related theme. These are arranged in a particular hierarchy that originated in the early 80s. Newsgroup names start with one of a series of broad topic names. For example, newsgroups beginning with '**sci**' should have scientific and engineering content. These broad topics are followed by a series of more specific topic names. '**sci.engr**' groups, for example, are limited to discussion about engineering subjects, and '**sci.engr.mining**' would be a group dedicated to very specific discussion on mining engineering topics.

There are many national and regional groups, including **uk**, but some of the main topic headers are:

| | |
|---|---|
| **alt** | Controversial, or unusual topics; not always carried by servers. |
| **bionet** | Research biology. |
| **bit.listserv** | Conferences originating as Bitnet mailing lists. |
| **biz** | Business. |
| **comp** | Computers and related subjects. |
| **misc** | Discussions that don't fit anywhere else. |
| **news** | News about Usenet and its groups. |
| **rec** | Hobbies, games and recreation. |
| **sci** | Science and engineering, other than research biology. |
| **soc** | Social groups, often ethnically related. |
| **talk** | Politics and related topics. |

With such an almost unlimited choice, you should very soon be able to subscribe to your own unique reading list of newsgroups. Subscribing does not mean you have to pay something, but means that when you enter News you will only see the groups in which you are most interested, and won't have to search through all of the others every time.

## Starting to Read News

Read News

Initially you start the News process from the Main window of Outlook Express (see page 92), by either clicking the **Read News** icon shown here, or with the **Go**, **News** menu command. This opens the Internet Connection Wizard for you to complete your details. Once this has been completed and you have subscribed to one, or more, newsgroups, you simply click on a folder in the Folders List to access that newsgroup. Our example on page 92 shows two newsgroups at the bottom of this list.

## Internet News Configuration

Before you can access the Usenet groups you must make sure that your details and those of your news server are entered into the Internet Connection Wizard. You will need to enter your name, your e-mail address, the news server you want to connect to, and how you will connect to the server (LAN, manual or by modem). If necessary, you should get the correct entry details from your Internet service provider.

In our case there only seemed to be one empty group provided by our server. If you get this problem, don't worry, there are hundreds of news servers on the Internet that allow you to connect to them without a password. You should be able to find some lists of them by searching for 'open news servers' with one of

the search engines. One site we found that worked well
for us was:

**http://www.halcyon.com/machey/hunter.html**

There is no guarantee that this site will still be active
now, but it did look fairly permanent. Open news
servers themselves do not always stay permanently
available though.

## The Newsgroups Window

The initial set-up procedure finishes by downloading a
list of all the groups available on the news server. As
there are well over 30,000 available to some servers
this can take quite a while. When this is done, a
window similar to ours below opens and you can see
what newsgroups are available to you. If you are
subscribed to more than one server, the **News groups**

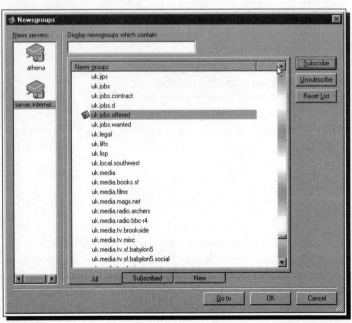

pane lists the groups available from the server selected in the **News servers** pane.

If you scroll down through the list of groups, almost at the bottom you should find some that start with **uk**. In our example, we selected **uk.jobs.offered** and clicked the **Go to** button, which is an easy way to have a look at the contents of a group. An easier way would have been to type 'uk.jobs' into the **Display newsgroups which contain** field. Only the five that matched this criterion would then have displayed.

A one line header (for each of the 141 messages contained in the group that day), was loaded into the Message Header pane, as shown below. Not too much unemployment in the computer industry!

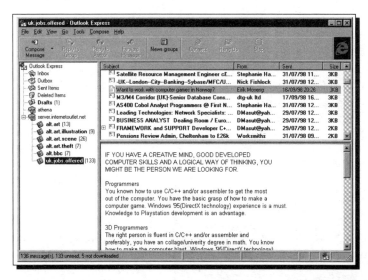

As soon as one of these headers is selected, the message itself appears in the Preview pane below it. This can take a few moments, don't forget it has to be downloaded over the network from your server.

## Subscribing to a Group:

If you think a group looks interesting and would be useful in the future, you should subscribe to it. To do this, locate it in the News groups window and click the **Subscribe** button. A newspaper icon is placed alongside the group name in the listing, as on Page 122. To remove a group from your subscribed list, you simply select it and click the **Unsubscribe** button.

Once you have selected all the groups you regularly want to keep tabs on, click the **Subscribed** tab button at the bottom of the list. In the future, each time you open the Newsgroups window, it will only display your chosen list. At any time while this window is open you can click **All** to see a complete listing again, or **New** to see any new groups.

## Adding a News Server

To add another news server to your set-up, open the **Tools**, **Accounts**, **News** settings box,click the **Add** and **News** buttons to open the Internet Connection Wizard, as shown below. Complete the details in the dialogue boxes as they are presented, entering the server name in the **News (NNTP) server** field. If this is

a closed, or a members-only type server, then complete the log-on details which you should have been given. Otherwise keep clicking **Next** and finally, selecting **Yes** to the last message box will download the server groups.

# The News Window

The News window, which is shown on page 123, is almost the same as the Main window we saw in the last chapter. It contains three panes, a Folders pane, a Message Header pane, and a Preview pane.

Clicking on a Newsgroup in the Folders pane, displays a listing of the group's current headers in the Message Header pane, which has four columns:

**Subject**     Shows the subject line of the message.

**From**     Gives the 'name' of the sender of the news message.

**Sent**     States the date and time the message was posted to the group.

**Size**     Gives the size of the file in KB.

You can sort messages by any of the columns and in ascending or descending order, by clicking in the column header. You can also add, remove, or rearrange the columns, and sort them, with the **View**, **Columns** menu command.

Clicking on a message header, downloads and displays the message body text in the Preview pane.

# The News Toolbar

 Opens a New Message window for creating a new e-mail message, with the To: field blank.

 Opens the New Message window for sending a message to be posted in the currently selected newsgroup.

Opens the New Message window for replying privately to the current news message, with the To: field pre-addressed to the original sender.

Opens the New Message window for forwarding the current news message. The To: field is blank. The original Subject field is prefixed with Fw:.

Opens the News groups window in which you select which news server to use and the groups to subscribe to.

Attempts to make a dial-up connection with the selected news server and to download selected messages or headers.

Breaks the dial-up connection with the currently connected news server.

Stops the current downloading operation. This option is only available when the download Status Indicator (on its right) is rotating.

## The Read Message Window

Double-clicking on a message header in the News window, opens a Read Message window with the message in it, as shown on the next page. This window has its own menu and Toolbar, and moving the mouse pointer over a Toolbar button shows what the button's action will be. Apart from the three icons described on the next page, this window is very much the same as the e-mail Read Message window in the last chapter.

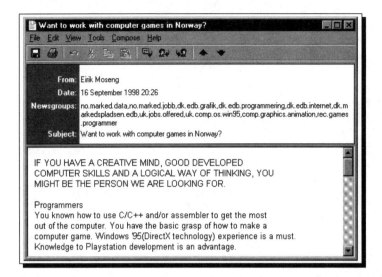

**Want to work with computer games in Norway?**

From: Eirik Moseng

Date: 16 September 1998 20:26

Newsgroups: no.marked.data,no.marked.jobb,dk.edb.grafik,dk.edb.programmering,dk.edb.internet,dk.m arkedspladsen.edb,uk.jobs.offered,uk.comp.os.win95,comp.graphics.animation,rec.games .programmer

Subject: Want to work with computer games in Norway?

IF YOU HAVE A CREATIVE MIND, GOOD DEVELOPED
COMPUTER SKILLS AND A LOGICAL WAY OF THINKING, YOU
MIGHT BE THE PERSON WE ARE LOOKING FOR.

Programmers
You known how to use C/C++ and/or assembler to get the most
out of the computer. You have the basic grasp of how to make a
computer game. Windows '95(DirectX technology) experience is a must.
Knowledge to Playstation development is an advantage.

## Replying to Messages

As long as you have chosen to **Make Outlook Express my default news reader** in the **Tools**, **Options**, **General** settings box, the News window Toolbar icons will use the Mail facilities to easily send messages of three different types.

 The **Reply to Group** icon addresses your message to the current newsgroup for all to read.

 The **Reply to Author** icon addresses an e-mail message to the individual who posted the current news message.

 The **Forward** icon prepares an e-mail with a copy of the current message, for you to address and complete.

Be very careful not to mix these up, the result could be embarrassing if you post a personal message to the whole group, for maybe millions of people to read!

## Postings Containing Pictures

If you have time to explore the many thousands of **alt** groups, you will find that a lot of them contain messages with picture files attached that are (or should be) relevant to the group name. Our example below shows one being downloaded from a group that does not normally need censoring, but be warned, most of them do these days! You never really know what you will find in them.

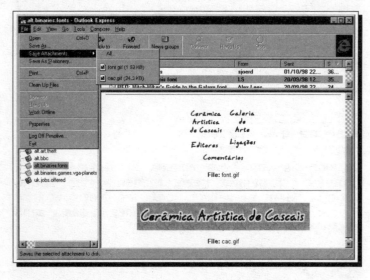

Clicking a message in the Header Pane will, as long as you are connected, download the message body in the Preview pane, and you will be able to view any graphics in the message, as shown above. When the image file has been completely downloaded, you can use the **File**, **Save Attachments** command to save any images in it to your hard disc.

Sometimes a paper clip icon is placed on the title bar of the Preview pane, as with e-mail attachments. Clicking this icon once will show the name of the attached file. Double-clicking it will open the actual file for you to look at. A very similar procedure to handling e-mail attachments. To save such an attached image to disc, hold down the <Ctrl> key when you click the displayed file name.

The same message is shown above, but this time opened in its own Read Message window, by double-clicking the message header. The image attachments are shown in their own pane below the message. To view, or run these, double-click their icons. As before, to save a file attachment, use the **File**, **Save Attachments** menu command, or right-click the attachment and select the **Save As** option.

## Threaded Messages

When a message is placed on a newsgroup, often someone replies and then a 'thread' of discussion is formed about the original message topic.

**News message icons**
The following icons indicate whether a thread (a topic and all of its responses) is expanded or collapsed, and whether messages and headers are marked as read or unread.

| This icon | Indicates this |
|---|---|
| ⊞ | This level of the thread is collapsed. Click the icon to show all the responses (expand the thread). |
| ⊟ | This level of the thread is expanded. Click the icon to hide all the responses (collapse the thread). |
| ▣ | The message has not been not opened. The heading appears in bold type. |
| ▣ | The message header has been marked read. |
| ▣ | The message has been marked read, and it is stored in a message file on your computer. |
| ▣ | The message has not been marked as read, and the header and body are stored in a message file on your computer. |
| ▣ | The message is no longer available on the server. |
| ✦ | The news message is marked to be downloaded. |
| ⊞✦ | The news message and all threads are marked to be downloaded. |
| ⊟✦ | The individual news message (without threads) is marked to be downloaded. |
| ▨ | The newsgroup is new on the server. |
| ▣ | The message is in progress in the Drafts folder. |

The edited News Help window above shows how you can recognise the Read and Thread status of any news message in the Message Header pane of a News window. Outlook Express messages are not threaded by default, but you can change this by checking the **Automatically expand conversation threads** option in the **Tools**, **Options**, **Read** settings sheet. Message replies would then always be placed with the original messages.

If you want the message list to display only the original message in a thread, select the first message, and then use the **View**, **Collapse** menu command, or click the minus (-) sign next to the original message.

If you then want the list to display all of a thread, select the first message, and then action the **View**, **Expand** menu command, or click the plus (+) sign next to the original message.

## Off-Line Viewing

If, like most of us, you are usually busy and don't have time to wait for long newsgroup messages to be downloaded, you can set up a batch download process and view selected headers and even whole messages off-line later on.

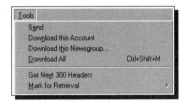

With the **Tools** menu options shown here, you can mark individual messages, threads, newsgroups, or even, heaven forbid, whole news server accounts, for downloading. In our example below, while still in the newsgroup alt.binaries.fonts, we have selected **Download this Newsgroup**, to open the box on the right. As you can see, there is a good choice of options.

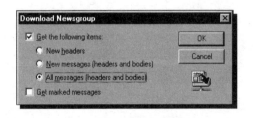

We could also have marked the headers of messages that looked interesting, before opening this box, and then to retrieve the messages themselves, selected **Get marked messages**. To mark a message this way, click its header, select **Tools Mark for Retrieval**, and then click **Mark Message**. You have to repeat these steps for each header whose message you want to read off-line.

Selecting **Download All** from the **Tools** menu, or from the Outlook Express opening window, causes the program to dial your Internet connection, if this is necessary, and to download the full messages for off-line reading. If you have been greedy with your marking, we hope you do not run out of disc space.

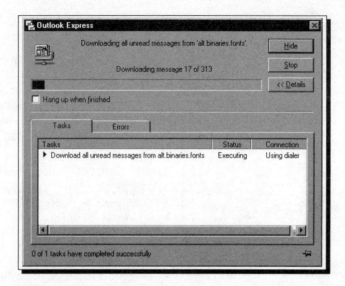

A downloading box, similar to the one above, will show you how the download process is going. If you are using a modem connection, you should definitely check the **Hang up when finished** option. Your phone bill will almost certainly be big enough already!

After you download messages for off-line reading and have disconnected from the Internet, you can return to the News Window and the message header icons, shown on the previous page, will show the status of any saved, or cached, headers or messages. Clicking the **View**, **Current View**, **Downloaded Messages** menu command, will display only the downloaded messages, hopefully, for you to read.

## Newsgroup Caches

Each newsgroup you subscribe to has its own cache file on your computer and everything you download from that group, either manually or for off-line viewing, is saved in this cache. When you select to view an item that is stored in a cache it is 'instantly' displayed, as it does not have to be downloaded. This is all very well, but if you are not careful you can fill your hard disc up with material you don't even know you are keeping.

## Controlling the Caches :

The **Tools**, **Options**, **Advanced** settings sheet gives you control of the size of all your cached message files, as we show in the dialogue boxes below.

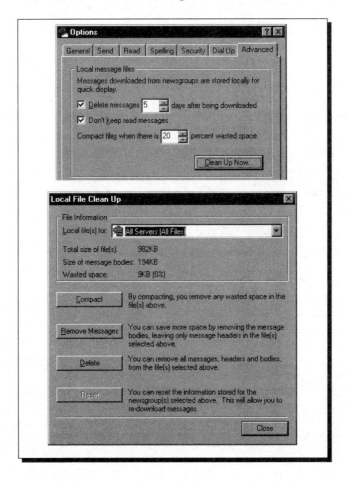

The settings shown at the top on the previous page will prevent things getting too much out of hand, but every now and then you should click the **Clean Up Now** button to open the box shown below it. Here you can manually compact, delete, or remove messages from all or specific message files, newsgroups, or servers. This clean-up procedure is usually known as 'purging.' The same 'manual clean up' options are also available from the News menu with the **File**, **Clean Up Files** command.

Purging unused, old, or large newsgroups can increase your free hard disc space enormously. Most news servers remove old messages and headers on a regular basis, sometimes even weekly. The next time you connect to a newsgroup you've purged, your cache is rebuilt with just the current messages and headers from the server.

## On Your Own

You should, by now, have enough basic knowledge to happily venture forth into the unknown.

Good luck, but please remember that there are millions of other newsgroup readers, and you never know where, or who, they are. Watch what you say in your postings, there is enough rubbish there already.

# 9. BEHAVIOUR ON THE INTERNET

As we saw in the first chapter, the Internet has grown up without any real control. It has grown, just like Topsy, but some of the behaviour you see there is not always quite as nice. We will not talk about pornography, or worse. If that is what you want, it is almost certainly there to be found (as in most major cities of the world), but increasingly now it is hidden behind closed doors. Most really dubious Web sites require membership and payment, but the Usenet groups are still a problem. If you have children that use your computer to surf the Web, the Internet Explorer has a security feature to enable you to control what they are exposed to, this is briefly discussed at the end of the chapter.

Parts of the media seem to have latched onto the idea that anything illegal or unusual that people get up to is because they saw how to do it on the Internet. It seems to have become something of a scapegoat. We have seen this recently regarding the making of bombs and the perpetration of credit card fraud.

The Internet does have its problem children, just like any other area of our society. Maybe one of the problems is just that, children. They seem to run wild in some of the newsgroups, posting all manner of objectionable and misspelled messages.

We will very briefly mention some of the more dubious behaviour patterns you may encounter on your way round the Internet, especially in the newsgroups, and to a lesser extent the mailing lists.

## Internet Flames

A flame is a particularly nasty, personal attack on somebody for something he, or she, has written in a posting. Newsgroups are notorious for flaming (burning people up). This can sometimes lead to long and drawn-out discussions on what really are stupid matters. These 'flame wars' can sometimes be fun to watch at first, but quickly grow boring, and become a general waste of everyone's time and mail space.

But, be warned, once you start posting to groups you may well upset someone, without even meaning to. If they are vicious, you may get flamed.

## Spam, Spam, Bacon and Spam

Spamming, on the Internet, is the practice of sending a message to a very large number of newsgroups and mailing lists. It is named after the Monty Python sketch, where you could have what you liked in the restaurant as long as it had spam with it. A spammer gives you little choice, you have to download his posting, but you don't have to read it.

It will not  be long before you encounter this 'problem' in some form, or other. Often a product, service, or a get rich quick scheme is being offered. We tend to ignore them and hope they will go away.

## Other Usenet Types

There are a number of other Usenet types you'll soon come to recognise, and love:

Ones that think their topic of interest should be forced on everyone else as frequently as possible. Often posting dozens of messages to unrelated groups, sometimes with ethnic contents.

Ones that take pages of message to get nowhere. This often includes excessive quoting by including the entire message in their reply, rather than deleting the irrelevant portions.

Ones who enjoy insulting others and post nasty, or even obscene, messages in unrelated newsgroups.

Ones who include enormous signatures at the end of their postings, often including enormous text graphics. These are harmless, but can be annoying.

Not really in the same category, but the term 'lurker' is commonly used and needs some explanation. It usually seems to be used derogatively, but we do not know why. The best definition we have found is:

**lurker:**[1] /**n.**/ One of the 'silent majority' in an electronic forum; one who posts occasionally or not at all but is known to read the group's postings regularly. This term is not pejorative and indeed is casually used reflexively: "Oh, I'm just lurking." Often used in 'the lurkers', the hypothetical audience for the group's {flamage} - emitting regulars. When a lurker speaks up for the first time, this is called 'delurking'.

Most of us, and especially new users, must be classified as lurkers for much of the time.

## Some Internet Etiquette

Often called 'netiquette' the following list[2] makes good reading and should help you avoid most flames on the Net:

**1** DON'T include the entire contents of a previous posting in your reply.

DO cut mercilessly. Leave just enough to indicate what you're responding to. NEVER include mail headers except maybe the 'From:' line. If you can't figure out how to delete lines in

---

[1]  The on-line hacker Jargon File, version 3.3.3, 25 MAR 1996

[2]  Patrick Crispen's Internet Roadmap, 1994

your mailer software, paraphrase or re-type the quoted material.

2    DON'T reply to a point in a posting without quoting or paraphrasing what you're responding to and who said it. Reason: a dozen postings may occur between the original message and your reply.

DO quote (briefly) or paraphrase. If the original 'Subject:' line was 'Big dogs' make sure yours says 'Re: Big dogs'. Some REPLY functions do this automatically. By net convention, included lines are preceded by '>' (greater-than signs). Some mail editors and newsreaders do this automatically. Others require you to do it manually or set the 'indent character' to '>'.

At some sites your reply may get there before the original.

3    DON'T send a message saying "Why doesn't anybody say anything about X?"

It's always a risk to start a new topic (often called a thread). The group may have just finished a long, bitter war about that very subject. But if you want to take the risk, SAY SOMETHING yourself about the subject.

4    DON'T send lines longer than 70 characters. This is a kindness to folks with terminal-based mail editors or newsreaders. Some mail gateways truncate extra characters turning your deathless prose into gibberish.

Some mail editor tools only SEEM to insert line breaks for you, but actually don't, so that every paragraph is one immense line. Learn what your mail editor does.

**5** DON'T SEND A MESSAGE IN ALL CAPS. CAPITALISED MESSAGES ARE HARDER TO READ THAN LOWER CASE OR MIXED CASE.

DO use normal capitalisation. Separate your paragraphs with blank lines. Make your message inviting to your potential readers.

**6** DON'T betray confidences. It is all too easy to quote a personal letter in a posting to the entire group.

DO read the 'To:' and 'Cc:' lines in your message before you send it. Are you SURE you want the mail to go there?

**7** DON'T make statements which can be interpreted as official positions of your organisation or offers to do business. Saying "Boy, I'd sure like to have one of them Crays" could result in a truck at your loading dock and a bill in the mail even larger than a student loan.

DO treat every post as though you were sending a copy to your boss, your minister, and your worst enemy.

**8** DON'T rely on the ability of your readers to tell the difference between serious statements and satire, or sarcasm. It's hard to write funny. It's even harder to write satire.

DO remember that no one can hear your tone of voice. Use smileys, like:

**:-)** or **;^)**

turn your head anti-clockwise to see the smile.

You can also use capitals for emphasis, or use Net conventions for italics and underlines as in:

"You said the guitar solo on "Comfortably Numb" from Pink Floyd's, The Wall, was *lame*? Are you OUT OF YOUR MIND???!!!"

**9** DON'T make a posting that says nothing but "Me, too." This is most annoying when combined with (1) or (2) above. Another one is "I don't know."

DO remember the immortal words of Martin Farquhar Tupper (1810-1889): "*Well-timed silence hath more eloquence than speech.*"

## Censoring Your Web Browser

The Internet Explorer allows you to control what Web sites your children can access. This is located on the **View**, **Internet Options**, **Content** settings sheet shown here.

Clicking the **Enable** button will ask you to establish a password. You have to do this before you can go any further, but please don't forget it or you will find yourself re-installing the Explorer in the future!

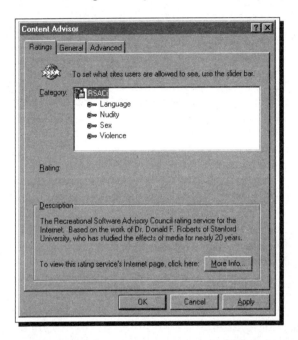

The Content Adviser control window is then opened, as shown above, which has four sliders to allow you to set the degree of language, nudity, sex and violence you want your children (or other users) to be exposed to.

This facility depends on Web sites having a rating system 'attached to them'. The Content Adviser then filters out unsuitable sites and prohibits access to them. The default site rating service is provided by the Recreational Software Advisory Council. There is the facility to select others in the **Advanced** tab section.

By default, if a Web site does not have a rating your users will not be able to access it. They will be presented with a blacked out screen if they try. You can alter this, however, in the **General** tab section, by checking the **Users can see sites that have no rating** option. Also in this section you can use the **Change Password** feature.

When you have made all the settings you want, press **OK** enough times to close the Content Adviser. You have now censored your computer, probably for the first time!

To cancel, or change, your security settings in the future, open the **View**, **Internet Options**, **Content** sheet and click the **Disable** button. You will need your password to access the Content Adviser.

This measure could also be usefully used by organisations to limit their personnel to specific sites on the Internet. This would not be a popular measure, but would almost certainly reduce the amount of wasted time.

## Still a Feature for the Future:

We feel this feature is a commendable attempt by Microsoft to make surfing the Web a safer place for your children, but it does depend on all the 'non-exotic' sites getting rated. At the moment this is anything but the case, as one of Microsoft's pages recently stated that 50,000 sites were signed up. With Content Adviser enabled you may as well turn off your computer, or cancel your Internet Service agreement, at least.

# 10. GLOSSARY OF TERMS

Add-in
A mini-program which runs in conjunction with a web browser and enhances its functionality.

Address
A unique number or name that identifies a specific computer or user on a network.

Anonymous FTP
Anonymous FTP allows you to connect to a remote computer and transfer public files back to your local computer without the need to have a user ID and password.

Application
Software (program) designed to carry out certain activity, such as word processing.

Applet
A program that can be downloaded over a network and launched on the user's computer.

Archie
Archie is an Internet service that allows you to locate files that can be downloaded via FTP.

Association
An identification of a filename extension to a program. This lets Windows open the program when its files are selected.

ASCII
A binary code representation of a character set. The name stands for 'American Standard Code for Information Interchange'.

Authoring
The process of creating web documents or software.

Backbone
The main transmission lines of the Internet, running at over 45Mbps.

| | |
|---|---|
| Backup | To make a back-up copy of a file or a disc for safekeeping. |
| Bandwidth | The range of transmission frequencies a network can use. The greater the bandwidth the more information that can be transferred over a network. |
| Banner | An advertising graphic shown on a Web page. |
| BBS | Bulletin Board System, a computer equipped with software and telecoms links that allow it to act as an information host for remote computer systems. |
| BinHex | A file conversion format that converts binary files to ASCII text files. |
| Bitmap | A technique for managing the image displayed on a computer screen. |
| Bookmarks | A list of 'favourite' places used for quick access from a browser. |
| Browse | A button in some Windows dialogue boxes that lets you view a list of files and folders before you make a selection. |
| Browser | A program, like the Internet Explorer, that lets you graphically view Web pages. |
| Cache | An area of memory, or disc space, reserved for data, which speeds up down-loading. |
| Card | A removable printed-circuit board that is plugged into a computer expansion slot. |

| | |
|---|---|
| CD-ROM | Compact Disc - Read Only Memory; an optical disc which information may be read from but not written to. |
| CGI | Common Gateway Interface - a convention for servers to communicate with local applications and allow users to provide information to scripts attached to web pages, usually through forms. |
| cgi-bin | The most common name of a directory on a web server in which CGI programs are stored. |
| Client | A computer that has access to services over a computer network. The computer providing the services is a server. |
| Client application | A Windows application that can accept linked, or embedded, objects. |
| Clipboard | A temporary storage area of memory, where text and graphics are stored with the Windows cut and copy actions. |
| Command | An instruction given to a computer to carry out a particular action. |
| Compressed files | One that is compacted to save server space and reduce transfer times. Typical file extensions for compressed files include zip (DOS/Windows) and tar (UNIX). |
| Configuration | A general purpose term referring to the way you have your computer set up. |

| | |
|---|---|
| Cookies | Files stored on your hard drive by your Web browser that hold information for it to use. |
| CPU | The Central Processing Unit; the main chip that executes all instructions entered into a computer. |
| Cybercafe | Establishment with both coffee and Internet access for sale. |
| Cyberspace | Originated by William Gibson in his novel 'Neuromancer', now used to describe the Internet and the other computer networks. |
| Dial-up Connection | A popular form of Net connection for the home user, over standard telephone lines. |
| Direct Connection | A permanent connection between your computer system and the Internet. |
| Default | The command, device or option automatically chosen. |
| Desktop | The Windows screen working background, on which you place icons, folders, etc. |
| Device driver | A special file that must be loaded into memory for Windows to be able to address a specific procedure or hardware device. |
| Device name | A logical name used by DOS to identify a device, such as LPT1 or COM1 for the parallel or serial printer. |
| Dialogue box | A window displayed on the screen to allow the user to enter information. |

| | |
|---|---|
| Directory | An area on disc where information relating to a group of files is kept. Also known as a folder. |
| Disc | A device on which you can store programs and data. |
| Disconnect | To detach a drive, port or computer from a shared device, or to break an Internet connection. |
| Document | When used in reference to the Web, a document is any file containing text, media or hyperlinks that can be transferred from an HTTP server to a browser. Otherwise it is a file produced by an application program. |
| Domain | A group of devices, servers and computers on a network. |
| Domain Name | The name of an Internet site, for example www.michaelstrang.com, which allows you to reference Internet sites without knowing their true numerical address. |
| DOS | Disc Operating System. A collection of small specialised programs that allow interaction between user and computer. |
| Double-click | To quickly press and release a mouse button twice. |
| Download | To transfer to your computer a file, or data, from another computer. |
| DPI | Dots Per Inch - a resolution standard for laser printers. |

| | |
|---|---|
| Drag | To move an object on the screen by pressing and holding down the left mouse button while moving the mouse. |
| Drive name | The letter followed by a colon which identifies a floppy or hard disc drive. |
| EISA | Extended Industry Standard Architecture, for construction of PCs with the Intel 32-bit micro-processor. |
| Embedded object | Information in a document that is 'copied' from its source application. Selecting the object opens the creating application from within the document. |
| Engine | Software used by search services. |
| E-mail | Electronic Mail - A system that allows computer users to send and receive messages electronically. |
| Ethernet | A very common method of networking computers in a LAN. |
| FAQ | Frequently Asked Questions - A common feature on the Internet, FAQs are files of answers to commonly asked questions. |
| FAT | The File Allocation Table. An area on disc where information is kept on which part of the disc a file is located. |
| File extension | The optional suffix following the period in a filename. Windows |

uses this to identify the source application program.

| | |
|---|---|
| Filename | The name given to a file. In Windows 95+ this can be up to 256 characters long. |
| Firewall | Security measures designed to protect a networked system from unauthorised access. |
| Floppy disc | A removable disc on which information can be stored magnetically. |
| Folder | An area used to store a group of files, usually with a common link. |
| Flame | An insulting message exchanged via e-mail or within newsgroups. |
| Font | A graphic design representing a set of characters, numbers and symbols. |
| Freeware | Software that is available for downloading and unlimited use without charge. |
| FTP | File Transfer Protocol. The procedure for connecting to a remote computer and transferring files. |
| Function key | One of the series of 10 or 12 keys marked with the letter F and a numeral, used for specific operations. |
| Gateway | A computer system that allows otherwise incompatible networks to communicate with each other. |

| | |
|---|---|
| GIF | Graphics Interchange Format, a common standard for images on the Web. |
| Gopher | A text oriented, hierarchically organised, tool used to locate on-line resources. |
| Graphic | A picture or illustration, also called an image. Formats include GIF, JPEG, BMP, PCX, and TIFF. |
| Graphics card | A device that controls the display on the monitor and other allied functions. |
| GUI | A Graphic User Interface, such as Windows 98, the software front-end meant to provide an attractive and easy to use interface. |
| Hard copy | Output on paper. |
| Hard disc | A device built into the computer for holding programs and data. |
| Hardware | The equipment that makes up a computer system, excluding the programs or software. |
| Help | A Windows system that gives you instructions and additional information on using a program. |
| Helper application | A program allowing you to view multimedia files that your web browser cannot handle internally. |
| Hit | A single request from a web browser for a single item from a web server. |
| Home page | The document displayed when you first open your Web browser, |

or the first document you come to at a Web site.

| | |
|---|---|
| Host | Computer connected directly to the Internet that provides services to other local and/or remote computers. |
| Hotlist | A list of frequently used Web locations and URL addresses. |
| Host | A computer acting as an information or communications server. |
| HTML | HyperText Markup Language, the format used in documents on the Web. |
| HTML editor | Authoring tool which assists with the creation of HTML pages. |
| HTTP | HyperText Transport Protocol, the system used to link and transfer hypertext documents on the Web. |
| Hyperlink | A segment of text, or an inline image, that refers to another document on the Web. |
| Hypermedia | Hypertext extended to include linked multimedia. |
| Hypertext | A system that allows documents to be cross-linked so that the reader can explore related links, or documents, by clicking on a highlighted word or symbol. |
| Icon | A small graphic image that represents a function or object. Clicking on an icon produces an action. |
| Image | See graphic. |

| | |
|---|---|
| Imagemap | An image which has specified areas hyperlinked to some other page or service. |
| Indexing | The process of analysing Web pages and recording the occurrences of keywords for later use by search engines. |
| Insertion point | A flashing bar that shows where typed text will be entered into a document. |
| Interface | A device that allows you to connect a computer to its peripherals. |
| Internet | The global system of computer networks. |
| Intranet | A private network inside an organisation using the same kind of software as the Internet. |
| IRQ | Interrupt request lines - hardware lines used by devices to signal the processor that they are ready to send, or receive, data. |
| ISA | Industry Standard Architecture; a standard for internal connections in PCs. |
| ISDN | Integrated Services Digital Network, a telecom standard using digital transmission technology to support voice, video and data communications applications over regular telephone lines. |
| IP | Internet Protocol - The rules that provide basic Internet functions. |

| | |
|---|---|
| IP Address | Internet Protocol Address - every computer on the Internet has a unique identifying number. |
| ISP | Internet Service Provider - A company that offers access to the Internet. |
| Java | An object-oriented programming language created by Sun Microsystems for developing applications and applets that are capable of running on any computer, regardless of the operating system. |
| JPEG /JPG | Joint Photographic Experts Group, a popular cross-platform format for image files. JPEG is best suited for true colour original images. |
| Keyword | A searchable term which can be extracted from a data set, such as a Web page, during indexing. |
| Kilobyte | (KB); 1024 bytes of information or storage space. |
| LAN | Local Area Network - High-speed, privately-owned network covering a limited geographical area, such as an office or a building. |
| Laptop | A portable computer small enough to sit on your lap. |
| LCD | Liquid Crystal Display. |
| Leased-line | A leased phone line that provides a dedicated, direct connection to the Internet. |
| Links | The hypertext connections between Web pages. |

| | |
|---|---|
| Local | A resource that is located on your computer, not linked to it over a network. |
| Location | An Internet address. |
| Log on | To gain access to a network. |
| MCI | Media Control Interface - a standard for files and multimedia devices. |
| Megabyte | (MB); 1024 kilobytes of information or storage space. |
| Megahertz | (MHz); Speed of processor in millions of cycles per second. |
| Memory | Part of computer consisting of storage elements organised into addressable locations that can hold data and instructions. |
| Menu | A list of available options in an application. |
| Menu bar | The horizontal bar that lists the names of menus. |
| Microprocessor | The calculating chip within a computer. |
| Microsoft | The world's largest operating system and application software development company. Home of Bill Gates. |
| MIDI | Musical Instrument Digital Interface - enables devices to transmit and receive sound and music messages. |
| MIME | Multipurpose Internet Mail Extensions, a messaging standard that allows Internet users to exchange e-mail |

| | |
|---|---|
| | messages enhanced with graphics, video and voice. |
| MIPS | Million Instructions Per Second; measures speed of a system. |
| Mirror Site | An Internet site set up as an alternate to a busy site; contains copies of all the files stored at the primary location. |
| Metasearcher | A search engine that simultaneously passes a user's query on to several other search engines in parallel. |
| Modem | Short for Modulator-demodulator devices. An electronic device that lets computers communicate electronically. |
| Monitor | The display device connected to your PC, also called a screen. |
| Mouse | A device used to manipulate a pointer around your display and activate processes by pressing buttons. |
| Mouse Potato | Those of us who spend too much time in front of the computer. Recently included in the Oxford English Dictionary. |
| Mozilla | Alias for the Netscape browser. |
| MPEG | Motion Picture Experts Group - a video file format offering excellent quality in a relatively small file. |
| MS-DOS | Microsoft's implementation of the Disc Operating System for PCs. |

| | |
|---|---|
| Multimedia | The use of photographs, music and sound and movie images in a presentation. |
| Multi-tasking | Performing more than one operation at the same time. |
| NCSA | National Center for Super-computing Applications. A US federal funded organisation for the R and D of high-technology resources. |
| Netscape | A popular browser manufacturer. |
| Network | Two or more computers connected together to share resources. |
| Network server | Central computer which stores files for several linked computers. |
| NNTP | Network News Transfer Protocol A common method of article transfer over Usenet. |
| Node | Any single computer connected to a network. |
| Online | Having access to the Internet. |
| On-line Service | Services such as America On-line and CompuServe that provide content to subscribers and usually connections to the Internet. |
| Operating system | Software that runs a computer. |
| Packet | A piece of data. The TCP/IP protocol breaks large data files into smaller 'packets' for transmission. |
| Page | An HTML document, or Web site. |

| | |
|---|---|
| Password | A unique character string used to gain access to a network, program, or mailbox. |
| PATH | The location of a file in the directory tree. |
| Peripheral | Any device attached to a PC. |
| Perl | A popular language for programming CGI applications. |
| PIF file | Program information file - gives information to Windows about an MS-DOS application. |
| PING | A program for determining if another computer is currently connected to the Internet. |
| Pixel | A picture element on screen; the smallest element that can be independently assigned colour and intensity. |
| Plug-and-play | Hardware which can be plugged into a PC and be used immediately without configuration. |
| Plugin | A helper application that runs within a Web browser, used to display data types that the browser cannot handle internally. |
| PNG | Portable Network Graphics, an extensible file format for the lossless, portable, compressed storage of raster images. PNG provides a patent-free replacement for the GIF format. |
| POP | Post Office Protocol - a method of storing and returning e-mail. |
| Port | The place where information goes into or out of a computer, e.g. a |

modem might be connected to the serial port. With the Internet, port often refers to a number that is part of a URL.

| | |
|---|---|
| Post | To send a message to a mailing list or newsgroup. |
| PPP | Point-to-Point Protocol - One of two methods (see SLIP) for using special software to establish a temporary direct connection to the Internet over regular phone lines. |
| Print queue | A list of print jobs waiting to be sent to a printer. |
| Program | A set of instructions which cause a computer to perform tasks. |
| Promotion | Informing the world of the presence of your Web site. |
| Protocol | A set of rules or standards that define how computers communicate with each other. |
| Push | Automatically update information on your computer when you log onto the Internet. |
| Query | The set of keywords and operators sent by a user to a search engine. |
| Queue | A list of e-mail messages waiting to be sent over the Internet. |
| RAM | Random Access Memory. The computer's volatile memory. Data held in it is lost when power is switched off. |
| Real mode | MS-DOS mode, typically used to run programs, such as MS-DOS |

games, that will not run under Windows.

| | |
|---|---|
| Register | To contact the supplier of software that you have purchased to give your personal details. |
| Resource | A directory, or printer, that can be shared over a network. |
| Robot | A Web agent that visits sites, by requesting documents from them, for the purposes of indexing for search engines. Also known as Wanderers, Crawlers, or Spiders. |
| ROM | Read Only Memory. A PC's non-volatile memory. Data is written into this memory at manufacture and is not affected by power loss. |
| Router | A communications device used to transmit over a network via the most efficient route possible. |
| Screen saver | A display program that moves images on an inactive screen. |
| Scroll bar | A bar that appears at the right side or bottom edge of a window. |
| Search | Submit a query to a search engine. |
| Search engine | A program that helps users find information across the Internet. |
| Serial interface | An interface that transfers data as individual bits. |
| Server | A computer system that manages and delivers information for client computers. |
| SGML | Standard Generalised Markup Language. An SGML document |

consists of data characters and markup; the markup describes the structure of the information and an instance of that structure.

**Shared resource**  Any device, program or file that is available to network users.

**Shareware**  Software that is available on public networks and bulletin boards. Users are expected to pay a nominal amount to the software developer.

**Signature file**  An ASCII text file, maintained within e-mail programs, that contains text for your signature.

**Site**  A place on the Internet. Every Web page has a location where it resides which is called its site.

**SLIP**  Serial Line Internet Protocol, a method of Internet connection that enables computers to use phone lines and a modem to connect to the Internet without having to connect to a host.

**SMTP**  Simple Mail Transfer Protocol - a protocol dictating how e-mail messages are exchanged over the Internet.

**Snail mail**  Ordinary paper mail sent through a post office.

**Socket**  An endpoint for sending and receiving data between computers.

**Software**  The programs and instructions that control your PC.

**Spamming**  Sending the same message to a large number of mailing lists or newsgroups. Also to overload a Web page with excessive keywords in an attempt to get a better search ranking.

| | |
|---|---|
| Spider | See robot. |
| Spooler | Software which handles transfer of information to a store to be used by a peripheral device. |
| SQL | Structured Query Language, used with relational databases. |
| SSL | Secure Sockets Layer, the standard transmission security protocol developed by Netscape, which has been put into the public domain. |
| Subscribe | To become a member of. |
| Surfing | The process of looking around the Internet. |
| SVGA | Super Video Graphics Array; it has all the VGA modes but with 256, or more, colours. |
| Swap file | An area of your hard disc used to store temporary operating files, also known as virtual memory. |
| Sysop | System Operator - A person responsible for the physical operations of a computer system or network resource. |
| System disc | A disc containing files to enable a PC to start up. |
| T1 | An Internet leased line that carries up to 1.536 million bits per second (1.536Mbps). |

| | |
|---|---|
| T3 | An Internet leased line that carries up to 45 million bits per second (45Mbps). |
| TCP/IP | Transmission Control Protocol/Internet Protocol, combined protocols that perform the transfer of data between two computers. TCP monitors and ensures the correct transfer of data. IP receives the data, breaks it up into packets, and sends it to a network within the Internet. |
| Telnet | A program which allows people to remotely use computers across networks. |
| Text file | An unformatted file of text characters saved in ASCII format. |
| Thread | An ongoing message-based conversation on a single subject. |
| TIFF | Tag Image File Format - a popular graphic image file format. |
| Tool | Software program used to support Web site creation and management. |
| Toolbar | A bar containing icons giving quick access to commands. |
| Toggle | To turn an action on and off with the same switch. |
| TrueType fonts | Fonts that can be scaled to any size and print as they show on the screen. |
| UNIX | Multitasking, multi-user computer operating system that is run by many computers that are connected to the Internet. |

| | |
|---|---|
| Upload/Download | The process of transferring files between computers. Files are uploaded from your computer to another and downloaded from another computer to your own. |
| URL | Uniform Resource Locator, the addressing system used on the Web, containing information about the method of access, the server to be accessed and the path of the file to be accessed. |
| Usenet | Informal network of computers that allow the posting and reading of messages in newsgroups that focus on specific topics. |
| User ID | The unique identifier, usually used in conjunction with a password, which identifies you on a computer. |
| Veronica | A search utility that helps find information on Gopher servers. |
| Virtual Reality | Simulations of real or imaginary worlds, rendered on a flat two-dimensional screen but appearing three-dimensional. |
| Virus | A malicious program, downloaded from a web site or disc, designed to wipe out information on your computer. |
| VRML | Virtual Reality Modelling Language. A way to describe 'worlds' that are displayed in three dimensions for the user to 'walk through' or 'fly over'. |

| | |
|---|---|
| W3C | The World Wide Web Consortium that is steering standards development for the Web. |
| WAIS | Wide Area Information Server, a Net-wide system for looking up specific information in Internet databases. |
| WAV | Waveform Audio (.wav) - a common audio file format for DOS/Windows computers. |
| Web | A network of hypertext-based multimedia information servers. Browsers are used to view any information on the Web. |
| Web Page | An HTML document that is accessible on the Web. |
| Webmaster | One whose job it is to manage a web site. |
| WINSOCK | A Microsoft Windows file that provides the interface to TCP/IP services. |
| World Wide Web | See Web. |
| Zine | An electronic magazine accessed through the Web. |
| ZIP | A compressed file format (.zip). Many files available on the Internet are compressed or zipped in order to reduce storage space and transfer times. Also used to name a proprietary disc drive that uses large capacity removable discs. |

# APPENDIX A
# KEYBOARD SHORTCUTS

The following keyboard actions are the standard shortcuts for working with Explorer 4.

## Web Browser Shortcuts

| *Shortcut* | *Action* |
|---|---|
| **General** | |
| **F5** | Refresh the current page |
| **Esc** | Stop downloading a page |
| **Ctrl+F** | Find text in page |
| **Ctrl+O** | Go to a new location |
| **Ctrl+N** | Open a new browser window |
| **Ctrl+S** | Save the current page |
| **Ctrl+P** | Print the current page or frame |
| **Enter** | Activate a selected hyperlink |

### Viewing documents

| | |
|---|---|
| **Alt+>** | Go to next page |
| **Alt+<** | Go to previous page |
| **Sh+F10** | Display object menu for a hyperlink |
| **Ctrl+Tab** | Move forward between frames |
| **Sh+Ctrl+Tab** | Move back between frames |
| ↑ | Scroll up a document |
| ↓ | Scroll down a document |
| **PgUp** | Large scroll up a document |
| **PgDn** | Large scroll down a document |
| **Home** | Move to the beginning of a document |
| **End** | Move to the end of a document |
| **F11** | View fullscreen |

# Keyboard shortcuts for Outlook Express

| *Shortcut* | *Action* |
|---|---|
| **General** | |
| **F1** | Open help topics |
| **Ctrl+A** | Select all messages |

## Main Mail Window

| | |
|---|---|
| **Ctrl+L** | Show/hide the Folder list |
| **Ctrl+O** | Open the selected message |
| **Ctrl+Q** | Mark a message as read |
| **Tab** | Move between window panes |

## Main and Read Message Windows

| | |
|---|---|
| **Ctrl+D** | Delete a message |
| **Ctrl+F** | Forward a message |
| **Ctrl+I** | Go to your Inbox |
| **Ctrl+M** | Send and receive mail |
| **Ctrl+N** | Open a new message |
| **Ctrl+P** | Print the selected message |
| **Ctrl+R** | Reply to the author |
| **Sh+Ctrl+R** | Reply to all |
| **Ctrl+U** | Go to next unread message |
| **Ctrl+>** | Go to next message in the list |
| **Ctrl+<** | Go to previous message in the list |
| **Alt+Enter** | View properties of selected message |

## New Message Window

| | |
|---|---|
| **F3** | Find text |
| **F7** | Check spelling |
| **Esc** | Close a message |
| **Ctrl+K** | Check names |
| **Ctrl+Enter** | Send a message |
| **Sh+Ctrl+S** | Add a signature |

| _Shortcut_ | _Action_ |
|---|---|

## Main News Window

| | |
|---|---|
| **Sh+Ctrl+A** | Mark all news messages as read |
| **Ctrl+J** | Go to next unread newsgroup |
| **Sh+Ctrl+M** | Download news for offline reading |
| **Ctrl+O** | Open the selected message |
| **Ctrl+Q** | Mark a message as read |
| **Ctrl+W** | Go to a newsgroup |
| **Ctrl+Y** | Go to a folder |
| **Tab** | Move between window panes |
| ← or + | Expand a news thread |
| → or - | Collapse a news thread |

## Main and Read Message Windows

| | |
|---|---|
| **F5** | Refresh headers and articles |
| **Ctrl+F** | Forward a message |
| **Ctrl+G** | Reply to all |
| **Ctrl+N** | Post new message to the newsgroup |
| **Ctrl+P** | Print the selected message |
| **Ctrl+R** | Reply to the author |
| **Ctrl+>** | Go to the next message in the list |
| **Ctrl+<** | Go to previous message in the list |
| **Alt+Enter** | View properties of selected message |

## New Message Window

| | |
|---|---|
| **Sh+Ctrl+F** | Find text |
| **Esc** | Close a message |
| **Ctrl+K** | Check names |
| **Alt+S** | Send a message |
| **F7** | Check spelling |

# APPENDIX B
# INTERNET FILE FORMATS

All of the file formats found on the Internet can be broken into one of two types: **ASCII** text files you can view with WordPad or Notepad, and **Binary** which contain non-ASCII characters and cannot be viewed.

We include here a guide to the most common Internet file formats with details of how some of them can be viewed, or played.

## Plain Text (ASCII) Files:

**.html/.htm**    The language in which Web documents are authored. File type is ASCII and requires a Web browser like Explorer for viewing.

**.txt**    An ASCII text file which can be viewed with Notepad.

## Formatted Documents:

**.doc**    Used for formatted ASCII text files, but also for documents created in Microsoft Word.

**.pdf**    Portable Document Format, a binary format developed by Adobe Systems, Inc. that allows formatted documents to be transferred across the Internet so they look the same on any machine. Requires a Reader which is freely available directly from Adobe.

**.ps**    A PostScript file is unreadable except by a PostScript printer, or with an onscreen viewer like GhostScript.

# Compressed and Encoded Files:

**.arc**
An old binary format for archiving and compression, which can be manipulated by several programs, but especially ZipMagic.

**.arj**
A binary format for MS-DOS machines, especially in Europe. You can use WinZIP, or ZipMagic.

**.bin**
A Macbinary II Encoded File requiring Stuffit Expander.

**.exe**
A DOS or Windows binary executable program or self-extracting file. Launched by double-clicking on the file's icon.

**.gz/gzip**
The GNU Project's compression program, a binary format most commonly used for UNIX and PC files. Use ZipMagic which handles this format the same way as Zip files.

**.hqx**
A Macintosh binary file that has been converted into ASCII text so it can be safely transferred across the Net. Use BinHex13 (binhex13.zip) on a Windows PC to un-binhex it.

**.sit**
A Macintosh binary file that has been compressed using the Stuffit program. Use Stuffit Expander for Windows.

**.sea**
A Macintosh self-extracting binary archive file.

**.tar/.tar.gz/.tar.Z/.tgz**

These binary files are often found on Unix-based Internet sites. ZipMagic handles all these formats the same way as Zip files.

**.uu**

UUencoded binary file. Used to convert binary data into text so it can be sent via e-mail. Explorer automatically decodes this type. You can also use WinCode to UUdecode files in Windows.

**.Z**

A UNIX binary compression format. Use ZipMagic to decompress and view files with this extension.

**.zip**

A common binary compression standard for DOS and Windows that uses the DOS utility PKZIP. These files can be decompressed on the PC with WinZIP, or ZipMagic.

## Graphics Files:

**.gif**

One of the most common graphics file formats on the Internet, it stands for Graphics Interchange Format. Explorer views these automatically.

**.jpg/jpeg**

A popular binary compression standard used for photos and still images. Explorer also views these automatically.

**.tiff/.tif**

A very large, high-resolution binary image format. You can use Lview Pro or PolyView on a Windows PC.

## Sound Files:

### .au/uLaw/MuLaw

The most common sound format (binary) found on the Web.

### .aiff/.aif

A fairly common Macintosh sound format found on the Web.

### .mid/ .rmi

Musical Instrument Digital Interface files.

### .ra

Real Audio, a new binary audio format, which allows you to play sounds in real-time.

### .wav

Audio for Windows, the native sound format for Windows.

## Video Files:

### .avi

Audio Visual Interleave, the standard binary video format for Windows.

### .mov/.qt

Common binary formats for QuickTime movies, the Macintosh native movie platform.

### .mpg/mpeg

A standard binary format for 'movies' on the Internet, using the MPEG compression scheme. There is an MPEG FTP Site that has a large collection of MPEG player resources for all platforms (Mac, Windows, and UNIX).

### .ra/ .ram/ .rm/ .rmm

RealNetworks, RealAudio, and RealVideo files.

All of these multimedia file types can be played by the Microsoft Windows Media Player, that was released at the same time as Windows 98.

# INDEX

# COMPANION DISCS

## There is no COMPANION DISC for this book.

COMPANION DISCS for many of the other computer books written by the same author(s) and published by BERNARD BABANI (publishing) LTD, except for the ones with an asterisk against their title in the list at the front of this book, are available.

**Make sure you fill in your name and address** and specify the book number and title in your order.

### ORDERING INSTRUCTIONS
To obtain companion discs, fill in the order form below, or a copy of it if you don't want to spoil your book, enclose a cheque (payable to **P.R.M. Oliver**) or a postal order, and send it to the address given below.

| Book No. | Book Name | Unit Price | Total Price |
|---|---|---|---|
| BP ........ | | £3.50 | |
| BP ........ | | £3.50 | |
| BP ........ | | £3.50 | |
| Name ............................... Address ................................. | | Sub-total | £............. |
| | | P & P (@ 45p/disc) | £............. |
| | | Total Due | £............. |
| **Send to: P.R.M. Oliver, CSM, Pool, Redruth, Cornwall, TR15 3SE** | | | |

**PLEASE NOTE**

The author(s) are fully responsible for providing this Companion Disc service. The publishers of this book accept no responsibility for the supply, quality, or magnetic contents of the disc, in respect of any damage, or injury that might be suffered or caused by its use.